PREFACE

Every generation must find its own way of looking at
its national heroes. The flood of books which pours
out over the decades about our great men is not due to
the continual discovery of new historical evidence, but
to our own changing values. We do not admire them any
the less, but we admire them differently.

That is why, when Cedric Messina rang me one day and
asked if I would write a play about Churchill at his
prime in conflict with his ring of generals, and through
them winning the war, I leapt at the chance. Churchill
dominated my childhood. I was brought up in the war
with those tremendous speeches ringing in my ears from
our crackling wireless set, and I can't read them now
without being greatly moved. Yet as the memoirs of his
generals and close associates began to appear in the
fifties and sixties, another side of Churchill began to
surface. It was a side many people would prefer to have
remained hidden, but to me it made him even more
interesting, more complete, more human, understandable,
accessible, his achievements all the greater.

In this play (for it is a play, not a drama-documentary,
documentary-reconstruction or anything like that), I've
tried to see Churchill from 1979, a magnificent, rounded
human figure, the greatest Englishman of the century, to
whom we owe our survival. Timothy West's performance
fulfilled this viewpoint superlatively, bringing out the
brilliance, the humour, the childishness, the rages, the
sentimentality, the vulnerability and sheer magnificence
of the man superbly. Alan Gibson, the director, brought
his matchless camerawork and pace to illuminate the text
- it is the seventh show we have done together. But the
greatest honours must go to the producer Alan Shallcross,
whose uncanny skills and unbelievably hard work held the
ship on course through some of the most difficult and
hair-raising production nightmares I have known.

Ian Curteis.

CHURCHILL AND THE GENERALS was first presented on BBC-2
Television on 23 September 1979 with the following cast:

Neville Chamberlain	EDWARD JEWESBURY
Edward, Lord Halifax	BERNARD ARCHARD
Winston Churchill	TIMOTHY WEST
King George VI	LYNDON BROOK
General Sir Hastings Ismay	PAUL HARDWICK
General Sir John Dill	PETER COPLEY
General Sir Edmund Ironside	NOËL COLEMAN
Duty Officer	ADAM NORTON
Police Sergeant	DESMOND CULLUM-JONES
Queen Wilhelmina	DOREEN UBELS
Clement Attlee	BARRY JACKSON
Paul Reynaud	JACQUES DUBY
General Maurice Gamelin	ANDRÉ MARANNE
Brigadier-General Charles de Gaulle	JACQUES BOUDET
President Franklin Roosevelt	ARTHUR HILL
Harry Hopkins	ROBERT ARDEN
General Alan Brooke	ERIC PORTER
Queen Elizabeth	AMANDA WALKER
General Bernard Montgomery	IAN RICHARDSON
Anthony Eden	RICHARD EASTON
General Sir Archibald Wavell	PATRICK MAGEE
General Sir Claude Auchinleck	PATRICK ALLEN
Churchill's Butler	DEREK ENSOR
Sir Charles Wilson	GEOFFREY KEEN
General George Marshall	JOSEPH COTTEN
Henry Stimson	ALEXANDER KNOX
Orderly	ALAN HALLEY
General Sir Harold Alexander	TERENCE ALEXANDER
Major-General Dwight Eisenhower	RICHARD DYSART
Senior Duty Officer	JULIAN FOX
American Orderly	DOYLE RICHMOND
General Maitland Wilson	ROBERT RAGLAN
Admiral Sir Bertram Ramsay	NOËL JOHNSON

The play was directed by ALAN GIBSON, and produced
by ALAN SHALLCROSS, with JACK LE VIEN as co-producer
for Le Vien International Productions. The original
music was by WILFRED JOSEPHS.

CHURCHILL AND THE GENERALS

a television play

by IAN CURTEIS.

British Broadcasting Corporation

For ALAN SHALLCROSS

who commanded the battle.

Published by the
British Broadcasting Corporation
35 Marylebone High Street
London W1M 4AA

First published 1979
© Ian Curteis 1979
ISBN 0 563 17803 5

Douglas Rae Management Limited
28 Charing Cross Road
London WC2 ODJ

Printed in England by Imediaprint

CHAMBERLAIN   Neville Chamberlain, Prime Minister
of Great Britain when play begins;
Lord President of the Council in
Churchill's War Cabinet; died
November 1940.

HALIFAX   Edward, Lord Halifax, Foreign
Secretary when play begins; continues
in same post in Churchill's Cabinet
until January 1941 when he became
British Ambassador to the U.S. in
Washington.

CHURCHILL   Winston Churchill, First Lord of the
Admiralty until becoming Prime Minister.

KING   King George VI, aged 44 in 1940.

ISMAY   General Sir Hastings ('Pug') Ismay,
initially Deputy Secretary (Military)
to the War Cabinet, a post combined
with that of personal assistant to the
First Lord of the Admiralty; on
Churchill's translation to the
premiership, kept the latter post,
and also became Churchill's personal
representative on the Chiefs-of-Staff
Committee. Best thought of as
Churchill's right-hand-man throughout.

DILL   Field Marshall Sir John Dill. Initially
vice-Chief of the Imperial General Staff;
succeeded as CIGS 27 May 1940, until
November 1941; then resigned and took
a sinecure. (Initially a General.)

IRONSIDE   Field Marshall Sir William Ironside
(initially a General), CIGS. Resigned
27 May 1940, and took no further part
in the war.

ATTLEE	Clement Attlee. Leader of the Labour Party. In Churchill's (National) Government, became Lord Privy Seal and Deputy Prime Minister.
REYNAUD	M. Paul Reynaud, Premier of France 1940
GAMELIN	General Maurice Gamelin, C-in-C of the French Army in 1940.
DE GAULLE	Brigadier-General Charles de Gaulle.
ROOSEVELT	President Roosevelt, in 1940 aged 58.
HOPKINS	Harry Hopkins, Roosevelt's close confidant; officially, secretary to the Inner War Cabinet and personal assistant to the President.
BROOKE	General Alan Brooke, later Lord Alanbrooke; in 1940 Commander No. 2 Corps of British Expeditionary Force, France; May-June 1940, C-in-C South East England in preparation for the invasion; June 1940, C-in-C British Isles. Succeeded Dill as CIGS November 1941.
THE QUEEN	Queen Elizabeth, in 1940 aged 40.
MONTGOMERY	General Bernard Montgomery. Corps Commander in BEF 1940, in France; then Commander Central Southern England (Brighton) against the invasion. August 1942, Commander 8th Army; 1943- Commander British Forces in European Invasion, under Eisenhower's Supreme Command.
EDEN	Anthony Eden, Secretary of State for War in May 1940; succeeded Halifax as Foreign Secretary and entered War Cabinet in January, 1941, on the latter removal to Washington.

VELL	General Sir Archibald Wavell, C-in-C Middle East until June 1941.
CHINLECK	("Awk-in-leck") General Sir Claude, C-in-C Middle East in succession to Wavell, June 1941 until August 1942.
URCHILL'S BUTLER	
LSON	Sir Charles Wilson, Lord Moran, Churchill's personal doctor.
RSHALL	General George Marshall, Chief of U.S. Army General Staff.
IMSON	Henry Stimson, U.S. Secretary of War.
EXANDER	General Sir Harold Alexander, C-in-C Middle East, in succession to Auchinleck on 18 August 1942, till end of war.
SENHOWER	Major-General Dwight Eisenhower. 1940-2, Chief of War Plans, U.S. Army; June 1942, Commander of American Army in Europe and North Africa (Op. 'Torch'); December 1943, Supreme Commander of Allied Operations in Europe.
LSON	General Maitland Wilson, O.C. the British Military Expedition to the Greek Islands.
MSAY	Admiral Sir Bertram Ramsey.

*****

1.   OPENING TITLES SEQUENCE

Parliament Square, 1979. TIGHTENING IN on the statue of CHURCHILL in N.E. corner.

MIX to FILM of Houses of Parliament in May, 1940, sandbagged and barricaded.

We FADE THE SOUND UP of the uproar of the debate on the vote of censure on Chamberlain, calling for his resignation with bitterness and vehemence.

During the following we SUPER OVER FILM a C.U. CHAMBERLAIN.

                         LEO AMERY (V.O.)
                         (in ringing tones)
        ... and I say to the Prime Minister,
        You have sat too long here for any
        good you have been doing. Go. In
        the name of God, go !

                         MEMBERS (V.O.)
        Go go go go to ....

                         LLOYD GEORGE (V.O.)
                         (at Opposition Dispatch
                         Box)
        The nation is prepared for every
        sacrifice, so long as it has
        leadership. I say solemnly that
        the Prime Minister should give us
        an example of sacrifice now,
        because there is nothing which
        can contribute more to victory in
        this war, than that he should
        sacrifice the seals of office !

                         MEMBERS (V.O.)
        Resign resign resign ...

The rise to their feet, chanting and waving order papers.

For the first time, CHAMBERLAIN wearily raises his head.

                              CUT TO :

2. THE GARDEN OF 10 DOWNING STREET

A peaceful sunny day, May 1940.

LORD HALIFAX, CHURCHILL and CHAMBERLAIN, who is
shattered and exhausted, sit together in the
sunshine.

All three hold teacups.

                    CHAMBERLAIN
            Of course, I cannot continue as
            Prime Minister. After such bitter
            condemnation by the House ...

Silence.

            Though I still cannot bring myself
            to believe that the Germans will
            attack. What is that bird ?

                    HALIFAX
            A wren, I believe.

                    CHAMBERLAND
            Is it ?

                    HALIFAX
            I think so.

                    CHAMBERLAIN
            Clearly I cannot command the
            confidence to form a National
            Government. And the only
            candidates to do so, are you,
            Foreign Secretary, and to a
            lesser extent you, First Lord.
                    (a wry smile, almost
                    a sneer)
            The newspapers say that the whole
            future of Western civilisation
            may depend on my successor.
            Histrionics, of course ....

He sits back, and drinks tea.

A long pause, both candidates apparently waiting for
the other to speak.

The Bird sings.

2.   (CONTINUED)

> HALIFAX
> (eventually)
> All parties have said they will
> serve under me, provided Winston
> and his friends give their support.

> CHAMBERLAIN
> And you have repeatedly said,
> Winston, that you would serve under
> anyone to win this war.

CHURCHILL remains silent.

> Is that still your position ?

No reply.

> Winston, I do not understand your
> silence. Usually I cannot stop
> you talking. Will you serve in a
> Government led by Lord Halifax ?

CHURCHILL stays silent. The emotional struggle to do
so is acute, and apparent.

The other two are mystified.

> HALIFAX
> (to CHURCHILL)
> This country could be facing
> annihilation, unless you agree.

CHURCHILL maintains his stony silence, but now the tears
are running down his cheeks.

A further mystified pause, then HALIFAX surrenders.

> It would be difficult for a Member
> of the House of Lords to be Prime
> Minister, in such a war as this.
> Leadership must come from the
> Commons.

Pause.

> CHAMBERLAIN
> Then I shall report the substance
> of this meeting to the King.

3. <u>INT. KING'S STUDY</u>

CHAMBERLAIN and the KING, who is forty four, shy but firm.

                    KING
          But he is so rash and
          uncontrolled !

                    CHAMBERLAIN
          Your Majesty, the mere thought of
          Churchill in 10 Downing Street has
          sent the War Office into paroxisms.
          Many of his own party are appalled
          at the idea.

                    KING
          Yet who else is there ?

                    CHAMBERLAIN
          No-one.

The KING crosses to a large map of Western Europe hanging over his desk.

The troop positions of the Western Front are clearly marked.

                    KING
          I find it astonishing, Mr. Chamberlain,
          that we have been at war for eight
          months. Nothing's happening.

                    CHAMBERLAIN
          A <u>twilight</u> war.

                    KING
          Yes.

                    CHAMBERLAIN
          Winston's phrase.

                    KING
          The onslaught will come, if it
          does come,
                    (points)
          when the Germans cross the frontiers
          of Holland and Belgium here, against
          our Expeditionary Force. Or here,
          into France.

                    CHAMBERLAIN
          Perhaps we could leave a decision
          till then, sir ? It may never
          happen.

Pause.

3.   (CONTINUED)

> KING
> The decision is made for us, if
> the Germans attack.

> CHAMBERLAIN
> Yes.

> KING
> (turning)
> Is Winston such a terrible idea ?

> CHAMBERLAIN
> He is always the 4th Hussar, charging
> the guns at full gallop. He would
> drive his Generals mad, telling them
> how to do their job. As First Lord
> of the Admiralty, he's impetuous,
> erratic, extravagant. He is widely
> distrusted.

> KING
> Why did he stay silent ?

> CHAMBERLAIN
> I think he believes that under
> Halifax, this country could not win
> the war.

> KING
> But under him, we could ?

Silence.

4.   <u>CHURCHILL'S UNDERGROUND BEDROOM</u>

GENERAL SIR HASTINGS (PUG) ISMAY working quietly at
Churchill's desk at one end of the room.

He is fifty three, quiet, tactful, full of good humour,
utterly loyal to Churchill.

CHURCHILL deep in thought, standing at the large map
of S.E. England on the wall.

> CHURCHILL
> (quietly)
> Pug. Pug. We have little money.
> Grossly under-equipped forces. No
> strategy to speak of. No generals.

4.   (CONTINUED)

                         ISMAY
              No, First Lord.

                         CHURCHILL
              Oh, some brave fellows, but
              antiquated, unimaginative. Where
              are the young generals who could
              win this war ?

                         ISMAY
              Killed in 1916, leading those
              pathetic little charges over
              no-man's land, waving a revolver.

                         CHURCHILL
              Not all of them !

                         ISMAY
              A few survived.

                         CHURCHILL
              And where are they now ?

                         ISMAY
              In the British Expeditionary Force,
              sir, in subordinate positions.
              About to do battle with the
              mightiest army in the world.

5.   INT. UNDERGROUND CORRIDOR/ANTE ROOM

Midnight.

GENERAL SIR JOHN DILL walking unhurriedly down, papers
in hand. One or two MESSENGERS about, very casual and
lacking in urgency.

DILL turns into door to anteroom.

GENERAL SIR WILLIAM IRONSIDE (CHIEF OF IMPERIAL GENERAL
STAFF), working at papers.

He is a huge man, forceful, sixty, fearless and outspoken.

DILL, his Deputy, brings in a telegram.

It is all very quiet and still and unhurried.

5. (CONTINUED)

                         DILL
            General Lord Gort reports German
            tank formations closing up to the
            Belgian frontier just after dusk.

IRONSIDE leans back and reads the telegram.

                         IRONSIDE
            It would be a relief to have some
            action.

                         DILL
            Yes.

                         IRONSIDE
            We'd lose, of course.

6. INT. CHURCHILL'S UNDERGROUND BEDROOM

CHURCHILL lies awake in his camp bed on the floor, in
the dark. His eyes are open.

TRACK IN across the dark room ONTO HIS FACE.

The Telephone SHRILLS by his bed, and he takes it.

                         CHURCHILL
            Yes ?

                         VOICE   (DISTORT)
            Boxfulls of telegrams from BEF-HQ,
            sir. At 3 a.m. the German 3rd and
            4th Panzer Divisions crossed the
            Belgian frontier near Maastricht.
            We also have first unconfirmed
            reports of a massive parachute drop
            on the Hague.

                         CHURCHILL
            The French Frontier ?

                         VOICE
            An aerial bombardment all down the
            Maginot Line, sir, few details yet.

                         CHURCHILL
                    (glancing at watch)
            Troop movements ?

6.   (CONTINUED)

> VOICE
> There's one report that they've
> penetrated fifty miles, to Louvrain.

> CHURCHILL
> (startled)
> In ninety minutes ?

7.   INT.   UNDERGROUND WAR ROOM/
> CHAMBERLAIN'S BEDROOM

CROSS-CUTTING between DILL and CHAMBERLAIN on
telephones.

> DILL
> (demonstrating)
> Our Expeditionary Force immediately
> advanced into Belgium, under Plan
> D. to fight alongside the Belgian
> and French Armies along the River
> Dyle. They are now coming to grips
> with the enemy on this line.

> CHAMBERLAIN
> The _entire_ British Expeditionary
> Force ?

> DILL
> All of them, sir. A quarter of a
> million men. The bulk of the
> British Army.

> CHAMBERLAIN
> I've called a Cabinet meeting at
> 8 a.m. Please be on hand to report.

8.   THE KING'S BEDROOM

Darkness.

The King's POLICE SERGEANT, shaking him awake.

> SERGEANT
> Sir ! Wake up, sir ! Sir !

The KING wakes and sits up.

8.   (CONTINUED)

                          SERGEANT
                          (cont'd)
               The telephone, sir. Queen
               Wilhelmina of the Netherlands,
               sir.

                          KING
               Nonsense.

                          SERGEANT
               Sir, please ! -

He hands him the telephone.

THE KING lifts it.

                          KING
               Hallo.

Faint LONG-DISTANCE VOICES on a bad line.

                          VOICE
                          (faint)
               One moment.

Click-click, then the voice of WILHELMINA, shrill and
weeping.

                          WILHELMINA
               Oh ! King George !

                          KING
               Your Majesty ... Wilhelmina !

                          WILHELMINA
               The Bosche are pouring in along our
               entire frontier, they are just
               slaughtering my poor people, machine
               gunning them, bombing them ! We are
               a neutral, a neutral ! I am in my
               sitting room, can you hear the
               bombs ? You must send us planes,
               I beg of you !

                          KING
               Your Government is surely in touch
               with our Expeditionary Force ?

                          WILHELMINA
               But they will be cut off ! The
               Bosche are breaking through the
               French lines, at Sedan !

9.   INT.   UNDERGROUND WAR ROOM

DILL and IRONSIDE, at a meeting of the War Cabinet.

CHAMBERLAIN presides.

> IRONSIDE
> The German Panzer Divisions have
> punched a hole in the French line
> here, at Sedan, and are streaming
> through into France in great force,
> on a South West Line.
>   (draws on map)
> Thirty divisions.

> HALIFAX
>   (horrified)
> Thirty ?

> CHAMBERLAIN
> To take Paris.

> IRONSIDE
> That is the direction they are
> heading.

> CHURCHILL
> And our own forces ?

> DILL
> We have ordered a withdrawal to
> preserve the line, to the Franco-
> Belgian frontier.

> IRONSIDE
>   (attacking CHAMBERLAIN)
> We are short of planes, tanks,
> anti-tank guns, anti-aircraft guns
> and wireless equipment. Compared
> to the German Army, we look like
> Indians with scalping knives !

> CHURCHILL
>   (greatly moved)
> The whole root, and brain, and core
> of the British Army, on which, and
> around which, we need to build the
> great British Armies that will win
> this war, are about to be
> annihilated on the field, or be
> led into ignominious or starving
> captivity, that is what you are
> saying ?

9.   (CONTINUED)

                              HALIFAX
              Will the First Lord -

                              CHURCHILL
                         (bangs table)
              I beg that the Chief of Imperial
              General Staff will answer !

                              IRONSIDE
              Yes, First Lord.

                              CHURCHILL
              Then what is our policy ?

CHAMBERLAIN gives a wry smile, almost a sneer.

                              CHAMBERLAIN
              This is no longer my decision. I
              shall be tendering my resignation
              to the King at the conclusion of
              this Cabinet Meeting.

MEMBERS digest this, then each in turn turns and looks
at CHURCHILL.

ON CHURCHILL.

                              HALIFAX
                         (quietly)
              You must start now, Winston.

10. NEWSFILM

The colossal power of the German Army pouring into
France, Belgium and Holland.

French and Belgian troops streaming away in front of
them, in complete disorder.

The BEF making an orderly retreat, abandoning only
their heaviest equipment.

                              CHURCHILL   (V.O.)
              I speak to you for the first time
              as Prime Minister in a solemn hour
              for the life of our country, and for
              the Cause of Freedom. A tremendous
              battle is raging in France and
              Flanders. It would be foolish to
              disguise the gravity of the hour.
              It would be still more foolish to
              lose heart !

11. INT. UNDERGROUND CORRIDOR

TRACKING with ISMAY down the corridor to the War Room.

The entire building has been galvanised into activity.
SENIOR OFFICERS, even ADMIRALS, are running to and fro
with papers; bells are RINGING, phones of every colour
are being installed by engineers at each corner.

CHURCHILL'S VOICE can be heard booming away from the
direction of the War Room.

                    CHURCHILL (O.O.V.)
          .... the proximity fuse, and necessary
          rocket projectors have hitherto not
          received the attention which is their
          due. Pray let me have a report on
          this within three days ....

12. INT. UNDERGROUND WAR ROOM AND ANTE ROOM

In the Ante Room, TWO SECRETARIES pound away at massive
typewriters, taking dictation, direct onto them.

The place is a mass of telephone wires as more cables
are installed.

People run in and out with reports and telegrams.

CHURCHILL is walking back and forth between the two
rooms, through the directly-connecting door, dictating
to alternate secretaries, reading reports, smoking and
walking up and down while his VALET tries to get him
into his morning coat and brush it.

He seems to vibrate energy.

                    CHURCHILL
          To the Minister of Aircraft
          Production. Kindly let me have
          a complete analysis of regional
          aircraft production, and cost
          and capability, by 6 p.m. today.

His VALET is trying to brush his coat as he walks about.

ISMAY has come up.

12.   (CONTINUED)

                              CHURCHILL
                           (cont'd)
               Ah, Pug, Pug, the King has sent for
               me again, to discuss the names I
               have proposed for my Cabinet and
               chief officers. I trust you will
               continue as my representative to
               the Chiefs of Staff committee ?

                              ISMAY
               I should be honoured, sir.

                              CHURCHILL
               Good, good. Have you seen the
               telegram from the Middle East
               Command ?

                              ISMAY
               From General Wavell, yes.

                              CHURCHILL
               Saying he will continue the fight
               should Britain collapse. I've
               replied that there's life in the
               old dog yet, aha-ha. He's a brave
               man, I should like to meet him.
               Tell me about those men in the
               BEF - our young Generals. Who are
               they, give me their names.

                              ISMAY
               There's a remarkable Divisional
               Commander called Alexander, still
               in his 40's. Then there's O'Connor,
               Dempsey, Bernard Montgomery of the
               3rd Division - not everyone's cup
               of tea. But I think he's got great
               promise. Brookie you know about.

                              CHURCHILL
                           (nods)
               General Alan Brooke.

                              ISMAY
               He's a magnificent military machine.
               A bit formidable. Fighting on the
               Belgian flank at the moment.

                              CHURCHILL
               I wish I was there, I wish I was
               there !

12.   (CONTINUED)

                              ISMAY
                    Then there's Ritchie, William
                    Morgan -

                              CHURCHILL
                    Write them down, give me a brief
                    summary of their careers and your
                    comments upon them.

                              ISMAY
                    Some are pretty junior, sir.

                              CHURCHILL
                    It doesn't matter.
                              (to VALET)
                    Oh, stop it, stop it, leave me
                    alone.
                              (to SECRETARY)
                    Where is my cabinet list ? Tell
                    the BBC to set up their microphones
                    here, in this room.
                              (takes list and report)
                    I thank you.
                              (roars)
                    What bloody fool wrote this ?
                    Do you know, we invented the tank,
                    yet all we have in France is one
                    antiquated division of them ?
                    - One ? - Against an entire German
                    Panzer Army ?
                              (putting on his topper
                              and striding out)
                    The conduct of this war would be
                    very much improved if certain
                    generals were shot !

13.   INT. KING'S STUDY

        The KING is examining the short typed list of
        nominations for the War Cabinet.

                              KING
                    Chamberlain to remain in the Cabinet
                    as Lord President. And you propose
                    yourself as Minister of Defence as
                    well as Prime Minister ?

                              CHURCHILL
                    Giving me complete authority over
                    the entire war scene, subject to
                    Parliament, sir.

13. (CONTINUED)

                    KING
          But you would effectively be
          Commander-in-Chief, Generalissimo ?
          - with power to sack and appoint
          Generals ?

                    CHURCHILL
          That is certainly so, Your Majesty.
          We have no strategy: I shall
          propose strategy. We have few
          arms: I shall go to the Americans
          for arms. In spite of their non-
          intervention policy, I am certain
          their hearts are with us. My
          warnings to the country on this
          impending conflict over the past
          six years, have been so many, so
          detailed, and are now so terribly
          vindicated, I am sure that I can
          claim the aid of all. It is a
          magnificent position to start
          fighting from !

The KING holds out his hand to CHURCHILL, confirming
his appointment.

                    KING
          Mr. Prime Minister, I am glad you
          are so confident.

                    CHURCHILL
               (takes his hand and bows)
          My whole life has been but a
          preparation for this hour, and
          for this trial.

14. NEWSFILM

A sandbagged London, May 1940. Barricaded and
prepared for the onslaught.

Men and women going about their jobs in a curious
clam, the quiet before the storm.

                    CHURCHILL (V.O.)
          After the battle in France abates its
          force, then will come the battle for
          our island - for all that Britain is,
          and all that Britain means. And our
          task is not only to win that battle,
          but to win the war !

14.   (CONTINUED)

                        CHURCHILL (V.O.)
                         (cont'd)
              "Arm yourselves, therefore, and be
              ye men of valour, and be in
              readiness for the conflict !"

15.   INT. UNDERGROUND ANTEROOM

Ismay's office. GENERAL ISMAY is surrounded by hastily
erected military telephones and cables.

There is great activity, coming and going.

CHURCHILL'S VOICE can be heard booming through the
closed doors of the room itself.

DILL hurries in, with military telegram.

ISMAY rises.

                        DILL
              The German armoured thrust is being
              led by Guderian in person.

                        ISMAY
              Their tank expert.

                        DILL
              That's right.
                         (shows telegram)
              He preaches a savage cut through
              with fast tanks and armoured cars
              ... far into enemy territory, then
              a smart wheel and rush along behind
              enemy lines to cut lines of
              communication.
                         (he demonstrates on the
                          'current position' map
                          in the private office,
                          cutting the BEF off from
                          the sea)
              It could mean they're attempting to
              cut the entire Expeditionary Force
              off from the sea, like this.

ISMAY is astounded.

15.   (CONTINUED)

                    DILL
               (cont'd - indicating
                the double doors)
          They're still sitting ?

                    ISMAY
          Yes sir.

DILL crosses to doors of Cabinet Room and enters.

16.   INT. UNDERGROUND WAR ROOM

The first sitting of Churchill's War Cabinet. There
are only five members - CHURCHILL, HALIFAX, ATTLEE,
CHAMBERLAIN and GREENWOOD.

IRONSIDE is also present as Chief of the Imperial
General Staff.

As DILL enters, CHURCHILL is in the midst of an
harangue. His eager relish for the fight is clear.

                    CHURCHILL
          .... France is our bastion, if
          France should fall, there would be
          no buffer between us and the whole
          might and fury of the Wehrmacht,
          except the Channel. Should the
          French cry for help become desperate,
          I shall myself fly to France to
          discuss it with the French premier
          M. Reynaud -

Cabinet horrified.

                    CHAMBERLAIN
          But you can't possibly fly to
          France now !

                    ATTLEE
          Your place is here, Prime Minister.

                    CHAMBERLAIN
          Suppose your plane is shot at ?
          It would be extremely dangerous !

                    CHURCHILL
               (glare)
          In that case, I shall certainly
          fly to France.

16.   (CONTINUED)

                              DILL
                Excuse me, Prime Minister.
                (he whispers in his ear)

CHURCHILL startled. DILL continues.

                            CHURCHILL
                Guderian ? Is this certain ?

                              DILL
                Yes, sir.

                            CHURCHILL
                Ironside.

IRONSIDE and CHURCHILL rise, and the three of them go
into a huddle in one corner.

DILL demonstrates on the map which he showed Ismay in
previous scene.

                            HALIFAX
                Do we take it that this is an
                adjournment ?

                             ATTLEE
                Looks like it.

                          CHAMBERLAIN
                Then he should say so.

                            HALIFAX
                Will every Cabinet meeting now
                consist of a romantic monologue ?

CHURCHILL, DILL and IRONSIDE in a corner.

                            CHURCHILL
                This impels me to make changes
                faster than I had intended. You
                Ironside, have never hidden your
                dislike of being Chief of Imperial
                General Staff ?

                            IRONSIDE
                I'm a soldier, Prime Minister, not
                a pen-pusher.

                            CHURCHILL
                Ah-ha, I sympathise ! I shall suggest
                that His Majesty appoints you C-in-C
                Home Forces, to repel the imminent
                invasion of these islands. You, Dill,
                will succeed Ironside, as professional

16.   (CONTINUED)

                        CHURCHILL
                        (cont'd)
                Head of the British Army. So let
                us pray that when these positions
                are announced, there will still be
                a British Army to be Head <u>of</u> !

17.   <u>NEWSFILM</u>

        GUDERIAN's massive armoured drive across France,
        hurtling along at 60 mph. Little opposition.

A C T   T W O

18. INT. CHURCHILL'S UNDERGROUND BEDROOM

CHURCHILL asleep. He wakes as the TELEPHONE SHRILLS.

                    CHURCHILL
        Yes.

                    VOICE (DISTORT)
        Will you speak to the French
        Prime Minister, sir ? He's on
        the line from Paris now.

                    CHURCHILL
        Certainly, certainly, put him
        through.
                (Click-Click)
        Hallo ?

                    REYNAUD (DISTORT)
        Mr. Churchill !

                    CHURCHILL
        M. Reynaud. Good morning !

19. CROSS-CUTTING BETWEEN CHURCHILL AND
     REYNAUD IN HIS OFFICE IN THE QUAI D'ORSAY

                    REYNAUD
                (terribly distressed)
        The German break-through at Sedan
        has widened to fifty miles. Our
        army is in complete disorder -
        we are beaten, we have lost the
        battle !

                    CHURCHILL
                (eagerly)
        Prime Minister, listen. Such a
        massive thrust must exhaust itself
        soon - they must halt for supplies,
        and then we counter-attack !

                    REYNAUD
        But that is not possible ! You
        must send us more arms !

19.   (CONTINUED)

CHURCHILL sits up sharply.

> CHURCHILL
> Where are you speaking from ?

> REYNAUD
> My office in the Quai d'Orsay.

> CHURCHILL
> Wait there.

20.   <u>NEWSFILM</u>

A solitary British plane high up, and being shot at.

> DILL (V.O.)
> Paris in fifteen minutes, sir.

> CHURCHILL (V.O.)
> You mentioned a young General,
> General Auchinleck.

Flack explodes close to the plane.

20a. <u>INT. TINY PLANE (O.B.)</u>

ISMAY, DILL and CHURCHILL, who is working through papers.

The plane is small, noisy, rickety and unarmed.
It is wobbling violently from the flack.

> ISMAY
> I do believe that's flack !

CHURCHILL looks up, eyes sparkling.

> CHURCHILL
> Really ?

> DILL
> (going forward)
> We must be over the German
> armoured thrust.

> ISMAY
> Auchinleck is part of Home
> Defence Command.

20a   (CONTINUED)

>   CHURCHILL
> And so available for immediate
> interview ? Pray arrange it on
> our return. I wish to see Brooke,
> Montgomery, Gott, Gort, all the
> Generals - there is much to discuss !

More heavy flack. The plane wobbles violently.

>   ISMAY
> Some of them are rather busy, just
> at present, Prime Minister.

20b   EXT. GARDEN, QUAI D'ORSAY, PARIS

Piles of papers being hurriedly thrown onto bonfire.
Distant gunfire can be heard.

20c   INT. CONFERENCE ROOM, PARIS

A large, imposing room, dusty and in disorder. It
is very cold, everyone in overcoats.

CHURCHILL is at the window, with REYNAUD.

CHURCHILL is employing his excruciating French with
confidence.

>   CHURCHILL
> Qui brulent-ils ?

>   REYNAUD
> Des archives du Governement et
> des papiers secret.

CHURCHILL turns on him in amazement.

> Les Allemands vont prendre Paris
> dans un jour ou deux, nous ne
> savons pas des arreter !

The doors at the far end of the room open, and
TWO FRENCH GENERALS enter.

> Mr. Churchill, puis-je presenter mon
> Commandant en Chef, General Maurice
> Gamelin, et Brigadier-General
> Charles de Gaulle.

20c   (CONTINUED)

The GENERALS salute.

                    CHURCHILL
          Bonjour, monsieurs.

                    GAMELIN
          C'est mon devoir de vous informer,
          M. le Ministre, que les traverses
          blindes Allemandes ont atteint la
          cote a Abbeville a onze heurs du
          matin.   Ils avancent maintenant
          sur Boulogne et Calais.

CHURCHILL and REYNAUD are staggered.

          Voici ...
                    (he shows them on the
                    map)

                    CHURCHILL
                    (angry)
          Mais, mon General, ou and quand vous
          proposer your contre-attack ? De ici,
          or de ici, from the Sud ?

                    GAMELIN
          Je n'ai rien pour faire une contre-
          attaque.

                    CHURCHILL
                    (shout)
          Mais ou est your masse de manoeuvre ?

GAMELIN shrugs and shakes his head.

                    GAMELIN
          Aucune !

CHURCHILL almost gapes at him in disbelief.

                    REYNAUD
          Mr. Churchill, you must let us have
          more Spitfires, in great numbers !
          Then perhaps we can reform under
          air-cover, to counter-attack !

                    CHURCHILL
          But then we should have nothing at
          all with which to continue the war !

20c   (CONTINUED)

                              REYNAUD
                    If France collapses, England cannot
                    hope to hold out alone ! Here is
                    the decisive point, now is the
                    decisive moment. You ought not to
                    keep one single fighter-plane in
                    England !

                              CHURCHILL
                         (gathering strength)
                    This is not the decisive moment,
                    this is not the decisive point !
                    That will come when Hitler hurls
                    his Luftwaffe against Britain.
                    If we can keep command of the air
                    over our island - that is all I
                    ask - we will win it all back for
                    you. Our Governments have agreed
                    not to surrender separately to Nazi
                    force but if it is better for France
                    in her agony that her Army should
                    capitulate, then let her do so, and
                    leave the fight to us ! But whatever
                    happens here, we shall fight on ...
                         (banging table)
                    ... for ever and ever !

                              DE GAULLE
                    Si nous capitulons, comment pouvons-
                    nous faire cela ? Vous aviez perdu
                    votre armee et vos armes !

                              CHURCHILL
                         (roar)
                    We'll beat them over the head with
                    broomsticks as they crawl ashore,
                    if that's all we've got !

DILL enters.

                              DILL
                    Sir. Prime Minister. May I have
                    a word with you, sir.

CHURCHILL turns to him.

                    King Leopold has surrendered the
                    entire Belgian Army to the Germans.
                    I have double-checked, and it is
                    true.

                              CHURCHILL
                    When ?

20c   (CONTINUED)

                    DILL
          About forty minutes ago.

CHURCHILL grabs the map from GAMELIN.

          As a result, a thirty mile gap between
          the British Expeditionary Force and
          the sea has opened up, and the Nazis
          are pouring through. The entire
          British Expeditionary Force is
          trapped here, between the two arms
          of the German pincers. Gort has
          given orders on his own initiative,
          to make a desperate march back to
          the sea.

                    ISMAY
          It looks as if all those future
          commanders will be spending the
          rest of the war in German Prison
          camps, sir.

                    CHURCHILL
                    (pointing)
          We still hold Dunkirk.

                    DILL
          Yes.

                    ISMAY
          But we could only fight our way
          out of there now, by the most superb
          generalship in the field !

                    CHURCHILL
          If we have the generals who can do
          that, then we have the generals who
          could win this war !

22. NEWSFILM

The tremendous fight put up by the retreating BEF
against very great odds and heavy aerial attack.

23.   INT. PLANE

CHURCHILL, returning from Paris, scribbling the
draft of a letter.

CHURCHILL   (V.O.)
.... we expect our island to be
attacked both from the air and by
parachute and airborne troops, in
the near future, and we are getting
ready for them. If necessary, we
shall continue the war alone. But
I trust you realise, Mr. President,
that the voice and force of the
United States may count for nothing
if they are withheld too long ....

24.   STILLS

ESTABLISHING SHOTS or STILLS of the White House in
1940.

CHURCHILL'S VOICE OVER CONTINUES:

CHURCHILL   (V.O.)
All I ask now is that you proclaim
non-belligerency, which would mean ...

25.   INT. OVAL ROOM. WHITE HOUSE

ROOSEVELT at his desk, carefully reading the letter.

CHURCHILL   (V.O.)
... that you would help us with
everything, short of actually
engaging armed forces.

ROOSEVELT passes page of letter to HARRY HOPKINS, who
sits opposite, reading it as it is passed over.

Immediate needs are listed below -
tanks, destroyers, aircraft, anti-
aircraft guns and equipment, iron-
ore ... We shall pay as long as we
have the dollars !

26. <u>NEWSFILM</u>

Dunkirk. The evacuation of the British Army, under
tremendous attack.

> CHURCHILL (V.O.)
> Put your confidence in us, Mr.
> President. Give us your faith.
> Help us ! Help us ! Now we are
> alone !

The British army abandoning all its arms and
equipment, and scrambling onto the Armada of
Little Ships.

> The New World, with all its power
> and might, must step forth to the
> rescue of the Old !

ACT THREE

27. INT. UNDERGROUND CORRIDOR OUTSIDE WAR ROOM

GENERAL SIR ALAN BROOKE walks briskly down the long
corridor towards the door to Churchill's bedroom.

He is an alert, youthful looking man of fifty-seven,
immaculately dressed, with dark, aquiline features,
pokerfaced, abrupt staccato speech, clear decisive
manner.

There is a great deal of activity - MESSENGERS
hurrying about, telephones and teleprinters in
action, etc ...

CHURCHILL, in his famous siren suit, greets BROOKE
at the door to his bedroom, arms outstretched.

                    CHURCHILL
          General Brooke, General Brooke,
          how do you do !

                    BROOKE
          Good morning, Prime Minister.

Spontaneous applause and some cheering from the
office staff at the desks crammed along the corridor.

BROOKE is embarrassed.

                    CHURCHILL
          You see ? The Hero of Dunkirk !
          I cannot tell you how delighted
          we all are to see you safely
          returned from France. It has been
          magnificent, magnificent, though a
          trifle fraught at times. I trust
          you are rested ?

27.   (CONTINUED)

                    BROOKE
          I've had some sleep, thank you,
          sir.

                    CHURCHILL
          Good, good.
                    (ushering him in)
          General Ismay will be joining us,
          after the Chiefs of Staff meeting.
          By your actions, you have saved
          the entire British Army ....

28.   INT. UNDERGROUND WAR ROOM

          A Meeting of the Chiefs of Staff Committee.

          ISMAY, IRONSIDE and DILL are there, with other
          SENIOR OFFICERS.

          All are in uniform.

          ISMAY is in the Chair.

                    DILL
          We've got thirteen and a half
          badly mauled divisions out of
          France, and enough arms and armour
          to equip two of them. Plus a
          handful of fighter aircraft.
          Against that, the Nazis have one
          hundred and thirty magnificently
          armed divisions plus four thousand
          five hundred planes within ten
          minutes flying time of Southern
          England.

                    ISMAY
          The PM inspected the Kent coast
          yesterday - the most threatened
          coast in England. In one place,
          there were three guns to defend
          five miles of shoreline. One
          didn't work.

                    IRONSIDE
          I thought the Chief Rabbi put it
          rather well.

28.   (CONTINUED)

                          ISMAY
            Chief Rabbi ?

                          IRONSIDE
            The King asked him what he thought
            of our chances, and he replied:
            "It'll probably be alright, sir;
            but if I were you, I'd start putting
            some of the colonies in your wife's
            name".

29.   INT. CHURCHILL'S BEDROOM

       CHURCHILL and BROOKE lunching at a little table -
       a fine meal, with champagne.

       Behind them, the desk littered with work.

       CHURCHILL is glowing with relish and excitement.

                          CHURCHILL
            Two hundred and fifty thousand men
            saved ! - With little more than
            their socks, but no matter. An
            act of bravery which has rung
            around the world !

                          BROOKE
                       (embarrassed)
            I was only one of the commanders,
            sir. And it wasn't bravery, it was
            strategy.

                          CHURCHILL
            Your four exhausted divisions, against
            seventeen crack Panzer divisions ?
            Holding back a thirty mile flank,
            so our Army could escape ?

                          BROOKE
            Well, perhaps some bravery came
            into it -

                          CHURCHILL
            I should think so !

                          BROOKE
                       (firm)
            But it was mainly tactics, sir,
            strategy.

29.   (CONTINUED)

> CHURCHILL
> Humph.

BROOKE has instinctively hit on the right way to
answer CHURCHILL: firm, clear counter-attack.

CHURCHILL despises reasonableness, which will be
Dill's downfall.

> BROOKE
> The most frightful part was
> having to leave before one's troops.

> CHURCHILL
> I ordered that.

> BROOKE
> Yes.

> CHURCHILL
> We must preserve our commanders,
> our seed-corn of victory ! Your
> men were well looked after.

> BROOKE
> By Bernard Montgomery, yes.

> CHURCHILL
> Montgomery, Montgomery, tell me
> about him.

> BROOKE
> He's a bit of a maverick, but I've
> got great faith in him.

> CHURCHILL
> Bends the rules, eh ?

> BROOKE
> It has been known.

> CHURCHILL
> Haha !

> BROOKE
> Auchinleck had to give him a
> severe reprimand not long ago,
> because he'd found some way of
> pinching the best officers from
> other divisions, to build up his
> own.

> CHURCHILL
> And Alexander, I ordered him out
> too.

29.   (CONTINUED)

                              BROOKE
                    I saw him actually arriving on the
                    beach on an old pushbike, just
                    carrying his briefcase and revolver.

                              CHURCHILL
                              (delighted)
                    A pedal bicycle ?

                              BROOKE
                              (nods)
                    He disabled it before swimming out
                    to the boat. He fixed the front wheel
                    so that any German riding it would
                    fall and break his neck.

          CHURCHILL highly amused.

                    Of course, the sky was alive with
                    Stuka dive bombers, shooting us up.

                              CHURCHILL
                              (eyes gleaming)
                    And you were replying ?

                              BROOKE
                    With rifles, revolvers, anything
                    we'd got.

30.   INT. WAR ROOM

          Chiefs of Staff meeting continued.

                              ISMAY
                    Which brings us to the whole question
                    of General Wavell's position in
                    Egypt. With Italy's entry into the
                    war, his little army is faced with
                    immediate and massive invasion from
                    Libya.

                              DILL
                    Yet the PM wants to bring back no
                    less than eight of his batallions
                    for Home Defence !

                              IRONSIDE
                    And Wavell's said no.

                              DILL
                    Not so bluntly.

30.   (CONTINUED)

                          IRONSIDE
          But in effect.

                          ISMAY
                          (gently)
          He could be ordered to release them.

                          IRONSIDE
                          (turns on him)
          Then we would undoubtedly lose the
          Suez Canal and the oilfields, and
          the war, within a week ! Wavell is
          grotesquely outnumbered as it is !

                          DILL
          The PM must leave him alone.

                          ISMAY
          I shall report that to him.

                          IRONSIDE
          And tell him bluntly.

31.   INT.   CHURCHILL'S BEDROOM

                          CHURCHILL
          I need hardly tell you of the
          awesomeness of the responsibilities
          you are now undertaking. As
          Commander-in-Chief South East
          England, it is upon your shoulders
          that the whole might of the German
          invasion force will fall. But the
          whole nation is at fever pitch to
          get at their throats, you know !

                          BROOKE
          That's your doing, sir.

                          CHURCHILL
          Eh ?

                          BROOKE
          Your speeches. Magnificent. If
          there's one thing that'll save us,
          it's your voice.

31. (CONTINUED)

                    CHURCHILL
          Ha ! - A voice is a frail enough
          thing. I'm only saying what's in
          their hearts already. Anyhow, words
          are about the only weapon we've got
          at the moment.

MESSENGERS have been bringing in boxes and papers
quietly during this scene, and placing them on the
desk.

CHURCHILL concludes the lunch and rises.

          Study the situation at your new
          Headquarters. Come and see me at
          this hour on Thursday.
                    (offers hand)
          I must get to know my commanders in
          the field ...
                    (he keeps hold of BROOKE's
                    hand and peers at him
                    closely)
          Tell me, what do you do when you're
          not being a soldier ?

                    BROOKE
                    (after hesitation)
          Ornithology.

                    CHURCHILL
          Bird-watching !

                    BROOKE
          I can stand still for hours,
          watching a mother feed her young.

                    CHURCHILL
          British birds, I trust ?

                    BROOKE
          Oh yes. I shoot the teutonic kind.

                    CHURCHILL
          Haha !

Claps his shoulder.

                    BROOKE
          You must tell me the arms position,
          sir. Where can we hope to get
          enough arms, in such a short time ?

31   (CONTINUED)

> CHURCHILL
> I am making enquiries of an
> American friend. I will keep
> you informed.
> (leading him to door)
> We still have a week or two.
> The Germans must master the air,
> before they invade. But we must
> hurry !

32.   <u>NEWSFILM</u>

Sequence of the first massive wave of German bombers
and fighters approaching England to destroy the
airfields.

We hear the VOICE of CHURCHILL on the wireless.

> CHURCHILL   (V.O.)
> The Battle of France, is over.
> The Battle of Britain is about to
> begin. Hitler knows he will have
> to break us in these islands, or
> lose the war. If we can stand up
> to him, all Europe may be free and
> the life of the world may move
> forward into broad, sunlit uplands.

Guns blaze at the planes from below, and a few
Spitfires attack: but they are few and far between.

33.   <u>INT.   CHURCHILL'S UNDERGROUND BEDROOM</u>

CHURCHILL broadcasting. The microphone is suspended
a foot above his desk.

He leans forward, emphasising the next sentence for
Roosevelt:

> CHURCHILL
> But if we fail, then the whole world,
> <u>including the United States</u>, including
> <u>all we have</u> known and cared for, will
> sink into the abyss of a new Dark Age.

34.   INT. WHITE HOUSE. OVAL ROOM

ROOSEVELT and HARRY HOPKINS listening to the end
of the broadcast, on a massive wireless receiver.

ROOSEVELT (fifty-eight) sits in his wheelchair near
his desk.

HOPKINS (fifty) looks so frail and ill that a puff
of wind would blow him away. He is deplorably untidy.

                    CHURCHILL'S VOICE
          "Let us therefore brace ourselves
          to our duties, and so bear ourselves
          that, if the British Empire and its
          Commonwealth last for a thousand
          years, men will still say 'this
          was their finest hour.'"

                    ANNOUNCER
          That was the Prime Minister Mr. Ch -

ROOSEVELT switches it off. He has been much affected.

                    ROOSEVELT
          Incredible. Like the whole of
          English history come alive and
          blowing trumpets.

HOPKINS plucks up a letter from Roosevelt's desk.

                    HOPKINS
          At least he didn't go as far as he
          did in his letter.
                    (quotes)
          "If all else fails, the U.S. should
          immediately declare war. Only this
          can save Christian civilisation."

ROOSEVELT wheels his chair about in exasperation.

                    ROOSEVELT
          Sometimes he seems to have no
          political sense at all, Harry !
          I had to perform handstands to sell
          him the arms we have ! - with half
          America shouting that it'll all fall
          into Hitler's hands when Britain
          collapses and be turned against us.
                    (waves letter)
          And now he asks for fifty destroyers,
          six hundred aircraft ...

                    HOPKINS
          Have you seen the newspaper editorials
          about this ?

34.   (CONTINUED)

                         ROOSEVELT
          Don't remind me !

                         HOPKINS
          "Is Roosevelt leading us to
          disaster ?" "America says no to
          another war ?"

                         ROOSEVELT
          Do they think I want one ?

                         HOPKINS
          The point is you'll lose the
          Presidential election if you go
          too fast now - then you won't be
          able to help anyone.

ROOSEVELT stares out of the window.

                         ROOSEVELT
          What do you think of their
          chances, Harry ?

                         HOPKINS
          On paper, the British can't
          possibly hold out.

                         ROOSEVELT
          Apart from on paper ?

                         HOPKINS
                    (after thought)
          That's a leap in the dark. And
          there's only one thing I can hear
          there -
                    (points to wireless)
          - that voice.

ROOSEVELT turns and looks at HOPKINS, digesting this
remark.

Then he impulsively turns to his desk, scribbles
something on Churchill's letter, rings a bell.

                         ROOSEVELT
                    (jaw set)
          I'm going to send him some cigars,
          as well

35. EXT. BUCKINGHAM PALACE GARDENS. DAY

The KING is at revolver practice.

The QUEEN is reloading for him.

CHURCHILL is pacing up and down behind them,
agitated, banging his stick.

>   CHURCHILL
>   I cannot impress on you enough,
>   sir, the desirability of making
>   plans for your evacuation ! -
>   The first object of the Nazi
>   parachutists in Holland was the
>   Royal family !

>   KING
>   What do you intend to do, if there
>   is a parachute drop ?

>   CHURCHILL
>   Oh, I've got my old rifle under
>   the bed in Downing Street.

The KING gives him a twinkle, and fires.

>   (to QUEEN)
>   At least, Ma'am, let us discuss
>   the removal of the two princesses
>   to safety !

>   QUEEN
>   (peremptory)
>   The children can't go without me.
>   I can't leave the King. And the
>   King won't go.

>   KING
>   So there.
>   (fires)
>   How is your survey of commanders
>   going ?

>   CHURCHILL
>   I have met some, sir; I meet
>   Montgomery tomorrow, on the Brighton
>   sector, which he is defending.
>   (starts to glow)
>   Do you know, the whole of Brighton
>   seems to be armed with the most
>   original weapons, which he has

35.　(CONTINUED)

> CHURCHILL
> (cont'd)
> dragged up from somewhere - cudgels,
> pikes, pitchforks ... the Nazis
> are going to get the shock of their
> lives !

> QUEEN
> I do believe, Mr. Churchill, that
> you'd be rather disappointed if
> they don't invade, now.

ON CHURCHILL

36.　MONTAGE:　INT.　UNDERGROUND MAP ROOM /
　　　　　　　　　　UNDERGROUND ANTEROOM

Great activity.　ISMAY working at his desk.

MESSENGER brings yellow military telegram.

> ISMAY
> Thank you.

He reads it.

> 1st VOICE　(V.O.)
> "RAF photographic reconnaissance
> reports three hundred barges
> moving down canals towards the
> Danish coast.　Number of military
> vessels in Flushing harbour has
> doubled in twenty-four hours ...."

RED LIGHTS start FLASHING round the room and the
SIRENS can be HEARD STARTING UP outside.

He takes up a bright red air-raid report as it is
laid on his desk.

> 2nd VOICE　(V.O.)
> "Messerschmitt formations
> approaching the following sector
> airfields, Manston, Biggin Hill,
> Lympne, Uxbridge, Hornchurch ..."

Creep in NOISE OF BOMBING.

37. EXT. BRIGHTON - DAY

Establishing the Wartime sea front and EXT. ALBION
HOTEL, Brighton, 1940.

37a. INT. ALBION HOTEL

A large table in a bay window.

An air-raid is in progress, and bombing can be heard
fairly close.

CHURCHILL is with MONTGOMERY, who is fifty-three,
but looks younger; foxy, over-confident, devastatingly
philistine. Unlike any other General, he wears
ordinary battledress.

His forceful, nasal delivery and inability to pronounce
the letter 'R' accentuates his oddness.

CHURCHILL is tucking into a huge luncheon with great
relish. It fills his half of the large table.

In contrast, MONTGOMERY is picking at the odd bit of
celery and cream cracker.

                    MONTGOMERY
                  (very earnest)
        What I need most, Pwime Minister,
        is double-decker buses. We're the
        only fully operational division in
        the whole of England, ready to meet
        the Hun. But some fool in the War
        Office has made us immobile !

                    CHURCHILL
        I know.

                    MONTGOMERY
        We should be given double-decker
        buses, and held in strategic reserve
        for counter-attack !

                    CHURCHILL
        Shock tactics, eh ?

                    MONTGOMERY
        I've got tip-top troops, 100 percent
        fit. They run ten miles each day,
        every manjack of them. Women are
        not allowed, and alcohol strictly
        discouraged.

37a. (CONTINUED)

                    CHURCHILL
          I believe you make your senior
          officers run too ?

                    MONTGOMERY
          I do, sir. One of my brigadiers
          had a heart attack because of it.
          I said "jolly good".

                    CHURCHILL
          You did ?

                    MONTGOMERY
          Better to find the weak links now,
          I said, than when the Hun's at
          your throat.

                    CHURCHILL
          Hrumph. You're not drinking,
          General ?

                    MONTGOMERY
          I neither drink nor smoke, and
          I'm 100 percent fit.

                    CHURCHILL
                  (instantly)
          Well, I both drink and smoke, and
          I'm 200 percent fit.

    He opens another bottle of champagne.

                    MONTGOMERY
          I hope you're going to kick some
          of our useless Generals out, Pwime
          Minister. I could give you five
          or six examples.

                    CHURCHILL
          I really don't think you should
          talk to me like that.

                    MONTGOMERY
          Why not ? Plain speaking when
          alone, can't do any harm, surely ?
          Besides, they know they're useless.

                    CHURCHILL
          How do they know ?

                    MONTGOMERY
          I tell them.

    He munches dry biscuit.

37a.   (CONTINUED)

                              CHURCHILL
                    You must be a very popular man
                    in the British Army, General
                    Montgomery.

                              MONTGOMERY
                    I don't care about popularity.
                    I just want to win.

        ON CHURCHILL.

ACT   FOUR

38.   INT.   UNDERGROUND ANTEROOM

DILL and IRONSIDE having a sandwich lunch,
each at his desk.

> DILL
> The Prime Minister's talking of
> sacking Wavell over his refusal
> to send back those eight battalions,
> you know.

> IRONSIDE
> What ?

> DILL
> The eight battalions from the
> Desert Army needed for Home Defence -

> IRONSIDE
> Yes, yes, I remember, but ... sack
> him ?

> DILL
> The Prime Minister seems to think
> survival depends on being drastic
> about everything. I did my best
> to explain but ... he was in
> rather a temper at the time.

IRONSIDE glances at DILL: He looks shattered and
exhausted.

> I think we should at least persuade
> him to meet the man.

> IRONSIDE
> Bring him back from the desert for
> a few days ?

> DILL
> Yes.

38.   (CONTINUED)

                    IRONSIDE
          There's an Italian build-up on
          the Somaliland border, he shouldn't
          be away for long.
                    (pause)
          Who would replace him ?

                    DILL
                    (doubtful)
          Auchinleck ?

                    IRONSIDE
          Hmm.

                    DILL
          Brookie thinks very highly of him.

                    IRONSIDE
          It would be quite a shock, fifth
          Corps of Southern Command, to
          Commander-in-Chief of the entire
          Middle East.

                    DILL
          Not the only shock Winston has in
          mind.

39.   INT.   UNDERGROUND WAR ROOM

       BROOKE is facing EDEN, who is Secretary of State
       for War, now forty-three.

                    EDEN
          The Prime Minister wishes you to
          take over from General Ironside
          as Commander-in-Chief, Home
          Forces for the British Isles.
          You would become entirely
          responsible for repelling the
          German invasion.

       BROOKE astounded.

                    BROOKE
          What's happening to Ironside ?

                    EDEN
          He will retire on full pension.

                    BROOKE
          When ?

39.   (CONTINUED)

                              EDEN
                    In about half an hour.

                              BROOKE
                    But what about Lord Gort, the
                    commander of the entire BEF ?

                              EDEN
                    He is to be made Inspector of
                    Training.

BROOKE's head is swimming.

                    You will accept ?

BROOKE, still dumfounded, nods.

                    The Prime Minister will be very
                    pleased. You have probably not
                    yet seen the text of Hitler's
                    speech today. He makes the British
                    Government a "Final Offer", before
                    he ...
                              (he looks for the
                               exact quotation)
                    " ... unleashes on us a storm of
                    wrath and steel." Quite a moment
                    to take over.

                              BROOKE
                    Yes.

                              EDEN
                    You realise you will be seeing a
                    very great deal more of the Prime
                    Minister ?

BROOKE nods.

EDEN looks at him keenly:

                    And ... having to cope with him ?

40.   INT. CHURCHILL'S UNDERGROUND BEDROOM

Churchill's wrath on the news of Wavell's retreat
from Somaliland is appalling to behold.

DILL is attempting to defend him, but he is both
sensitive and ultra-reasonable, and CHURCHILL just
makes mincemeat of him.

40.   (CONTINUED)

CHURCHILL still holds the telegram.

                    CHURCHILL
                  (roar)
    Withdraw ? - Wavell has withdrawn
    from Somaliland - with scarcely a
    shot fired ?

                    DILL
    His men fought very bravely.

                    CHURCHILL
                  (waving arms wildly)
    Sack him ! Get rid of him !
    Our people at home are making the
    most heroic sacrifices unflinchingly,
    and what does he do ? - turn tail
    and run ?!

                    DILL
    Preserving the integrity of his
    tiny defence force against -

                    CHURCHILL
    You defend him because you're just
    as bad as he is ! The only thing
    you people defend, is your own
    skins.

                    DILL
    But you see, Prime Minister, they
    needed that little force to help
    defend Egypt. I must ask you to
    be reasonable about this ...

                    CHURCHILL
                  (banging table)
    We must have a victory, however
    small, however unimportant - we
    must show the Americans what we
    are made of, or we are lost.
    Doesn't Wavell realise just how
    close to the brink we are ?

41.   INT. OVAL ROOM SET.   WHITE HOUSE

ROOSEVELT sitting up in bed in pyjamas, reading
a cable, just a low bedside lamp.

                              CHURCHILL   (V.O.)
                    Former Naval Person to President
                    Roosevelt. It has now become
                    most urgent for you to let us
                    have the destroyers, motor-torpedo
                    boats and flying boats for which
                    we have asked ...

ROOSEVELT rubs his brow, a very worried man.

                    The Germans have the whole French
                    coastline from which to launch
                    U-Boat and dive-bomber attacks on
                    our merchant shipping. I am
                    confident that you will send us
                    fifty or sixty of your oldest
                    destroyers at once ...

ROOSEVELT reaches for his bedside telephone.

HOPKINS in bed, on telephone.

                              HOPKINS
                    They could pay for them in military
                    bases, not money.
                              ROOSEVELT   (V.O.)
                    What ?

                              HOPKINS
                    Suppose the British grant us 99-year
                    leases on, say, ten of their
                    military bases round the Empire,
                    wouldn't Congress accept that ?

                              ROOSEVELT   (V.O.)
                    They might. Oh, God ...

                              HOPKINS
                    None of us cares for walking a
                    tightrope, Mr. President.

                              ROOSEVELT
                    It's not that. It's just how
                    un-neutral can you get ?

42. INT. CHURCHILL'S UNDERGROUND BEDROOM

Defence maps of South East England spread out all
over the Cabinet table.

CHURCHILL sits at them, BROOKE stands and demonstrates.

                    BROOKE
          I spent today studying the
          existing defence plans as a
          whole.

                    CHURCHILL
          And you gained a clear idea of
          Ironside's thinking ?

                    BROOKE
          Yes.

                    CHURCHILL
                 (grunt)
          More than I ever did.

                    BROOKE
          His plan is the conventional
          one of linear defence in depth.
          Basically a static plan.

                    CHURCHILL
          Which you don't agree with.

                    BROOKE
          Swift offensive is the only answer.

CHURCHILL immediately lurches in his chair with
delight, and beams like a lighthouse.

          We should create mobile reserves
          near the coast to strike back at
          the enemy wherever he lands.

                    CHURCHILL
                 (twinkle)
          In double-decker buses.

                    BROOKE
                 (startled)
          What ?

                    CHURCHILL
          Nothing, go on.

42.   (CONTINUED)

                    BROOKE
          So we drive him back into the
          sea before he can consolidate.

He is put out by Churchill's audible gurgle of
delight.

          Is anything wrong, sir ?

                    CHURCHILL
          No, no. Now tell me, is there
          anything you need ?

                    BROOKE
          Everything !

                    CHURCHILL
          What ?

                    BROOKE
          Rifles, ammunition, Bofors guns,
          anti-tank guns, tanks ...

                    CHURCHILL
          And where on earth do you suppose
          I can get them from ? This is
          most ungrateful of you, General !

                    BROOKE
          Ungrateful ?

                    CHURCHILL
          After all I'm doing for you.

                    BROOKE
                (stumped)
          Er ... ?

                    CHURCHILL
          Great Heavens, no commander has
          been given the chance that I'm
          giving you now, since Drake faced
          the Armada ! Wavell is also asking
          me for arms.

                    BROOKE
          Couldn't the Americans help ?

                    CHURCHILL
                (innocent as butter)
          The Americans ? My dear General
          Brooke, have some consideration.
          Why, they're not even in the war ...
          yet.

43. EXT. WHITEHALL/HORSEGUARDS PARADE - DAY

EDEN with DILL. They are relaxed and get on well
together.

                    EDEN
          The PM's goading of Wavell has
          become intolerable. You saw his
          telegram on Tuesday, demanding his
          presence ?

                    DILL
          Yes.

                    EDEN
          He's never forgiven him over the
          Somaliland business. When does he
          arrive from Cairo ?

                    DILL
          Four p.m. by flying boat.

                    EDEN
          You know him well ?

                    DILL
          Oh yes. He's a great man. But
          I don't think Winston will have
          the faintest idea what to make
          of him.

44.   INT.   UNDERGROUND WAR ROOM

A joint meeting of the War Cabinet and Chief of
Staffs Committee.

CHURCHILL sits at one end of the table, and WAVELL
at the other, facing him.

WAVELL is fifty-seven, and is believed by many to be
the greatest of the Generals. He is quietly spoken,
often monosyllabic. His silences are proverbial.

One eye has been closed since he lost it in the
First World War trenches. The other watches gently
as he listens, missing nothing.

He is gentle, affectionate, loyal, vague, yet shrewd,
a mind which quietly darts to the point.

44.   (CONTINUED)

                         CHURCHILL
              General Wavell, we are extremely
              obliged to you for making the
              hazardous journey from Egypt so
              that we could talk over the serious
              events impending in the Middle
              East. We would be most grateful
              for your review of the situation,
              as you see it.

He sits back.

                         WAVELL
              That's a complicated matter.

A long silence.

CHURCHILL suddenly realises, with a start, that it is
all he intends to say.

                         EDEN
              Perhaps you would give us a
              summary of your main problems.

                         WAVELL
              Complexity.

Silence.

                         EDEN
              What ?

                         WAVELL
              The Middle East command is two
              thousand miles by eighteen hundreds,
              spread over two continents. It's
              an extraordinary mixture of military,
              diplomatic, administrative and
              political problems, of great
              complexity.

                         CHURCHILL
              But the Libyan Desert ....

                         WAVELL
              Yes.

                         CHURCHILL
              Are you confident of your position
              there ?

                         WAVELL
              No.

44.   (CONTINUED)

>   ISMAY
>   (hastily)
>   Perhaps you would refresh my
>   memory about it.

>   WAVELL
>   The Italians are building up their
>   forces and supply lines along the
>   Egyptian border and the road to
>   Tripoli.

>   CHURCHILL
>   Preparatory to invasion.

WAVELL looks at him, but says nothing.

>   Preparatory to invasion ?

>   WAVELL
>   Yes.

>   EDEN
>   What form do you anticipate
>   this might take ?

>   WAVELL
>   They may advance on a fifty-
>   mile front, turning our defences
>   at Matruh, and marching on
>   Alexandria.

>   CHURCHILL
>   And how will you repel this ?

>   WAVELL
>   As best we can.

Silence.

CHURCHILL is growing noticeably annoyed. EDEN
tries to cool it:

>   EDEN
>   Do you feel confident that you
>   could repel such an invasion ?

>   WAVELL
>   No.

Silence.

>   CHURCHILL
>   (snap)
>   Why not ?

44. (CONTINUED)

                          WAVELL
          We are fifty thousand against the
          Italian half-million. I am short
          of all the weapons which go to
          make up a modern fighting force.
          And it is weapons, not morale,
          which will decide this victory.

                          CHURCHILL
                     (with emphasis)
          No, sir !

                          WAVELL
                     (quiet conviction)
          Yes, sir.

                          CHURCHILL
                     (snapping)
          We in this island are outnumbered
          far more than ten to one, and we
          are even less well armed than you.
          Yet we do not falter !

                          WAVELL
          You've got the Channel; I've only
          got flat sand.

                          EDEN
          Where would you say, is your most
          vulnerable point ?

                          WAVELL
          Sidi Barrani.

                          CHURCHILL
                     (scuffling through papers)
          Your troop dispositions do not accord
          with that. I have studied them. You
          have the 4th and the 15th too far
          apart at that point, to take coordinated
          action when the Italians advance !

     WAVELL fixes his one eye on CHURCHILL, but says nothing.

          Well, what do you say to that ?

45. INT. ANTEROOM

     WAVELL sitting in a corner, quietly reading a book
     of verse.

     DILL is changing his shirt and tie.

     After a while, WAVELL looks up.

45.   (CONTINUED)

                    WAVELL
          He insisted on going over every
          one of my batalion positions, you
          know. His strategic sense seems
          to have got stuck about 1899.
          Mind, he's as brave as a lion.

                    DILL
          So are you.

                    WAVELL
          I don't roar, though.

Pause.

                    DILL
          You dislike him ?

                    WAVELL
               (surprised)
          I like him very much. How do
          you get on with him ?

                    DILL
          I have to bear his anger, his
          frustrations, his bullying, his
          sarcasm and abuse, for all the
          shortcomings of the army.

                    WAVELL
          Hmm. He doesn't know whether I'm
          any good or not. I see those little
          flecks of red come into his eyes when
          he gets angry. There's a tiny
          flower in the Western Desert just
          like that. Every now and then as
          you drive across those unbelievable
          wastes, you see those minute red
          jewels in the heat haze. Sometimes
          they're the only living things for
          a hundred miles.

                    DILL
               (after thought)
          If he heard you talk like that, he
          might begin to understand you.

WAVELL thinks about that, then turns back to his
book, expressionless.

46.   INT.   CHURCHILL'S BEDROOM

CHURCHILL and EDEN, over drinks.

                    CHURCHILL
                    (angry)
        He showed no mental vigour or
        resolve. He would make an
        acceptable chairman of a local
        Tory Association.

                    EDEN
        Many soldiers can't explain
        themselves.

                    CHURCHILL
                    (instantly)
        I always could. When he goes
        back, Anthony, I want you to do
        a Middle East Tour; prod him,
        goad him ... we must have a
        victory !

47.   INT.   WAR ROOM

Joint War Cabinet and Chiefs of Staff again, with
WAVELL. CHURCHILL, HALIFAX, BEAVERBROOK, ATTLEE,
GREENWOOD, EDEN, ISMAY, DILL and HEADS OF RAF AND
NAVY, with their POLITICAL ADVISERS.

CHAMBERLAIN is absent, sick.

                    ISMAY
        The Chiefs of Staff Committee
        has decided that, in spite of our
        own critical position, we should
        somehow send you more armaments.
                    (passes list to WAVELL)
        The chief item, as you see, is an
        entire batallion of tanks.

                    CHURCHILL
                    (growl)
        Which we can ill afford.

WAVELL takes the list and reads it in silence.

CHURCHILL is positively annoyed at the lack of
spontaneous reaction.

        Don't you say thank you ?

47.   (CONTINUED)

                        WAVELL
              History will do that.

CHURCHILL is unsure how to take that one.

                        ISMAY
              The question now, is do we send
              them by convoy all the way round
              the Cape in safety, or risk a
              quick dash through the Mediterranean.

                        CHURCHILL
              We must be bold, or nothing.

                        EDEN
              What does General Wavell say ?

                        WAVELL
              There's time to send them the
              safe way, round the Cape.

CHURCHILL glares at him, very angry.

                        CHURCHILL
              Caution again, General Wavell.
              Like your retreat from Somaliland !

                        WAVELL
                        (cool)
              A big butchers bill is no evidence
              of good tactics.

CHURCHILL nearly bursts a blood vessel.

48.   INT. WHITE HOUSE. OVAL ROOM

ROOSEVELT in his wheelchair, dictating.

                        ROOSEVELT
              Roosevelt to Former Naval Person.
              Can you give assurances that if we
              do manage to get you these
              destroyers, the British Fleet
              would be scuttled or sailed across
              the Atlantic to us, if the British
              capitulate ? Congress hung up on
              this point.

49.   INT.   CHURCHILL'S BEDROOM

> CHURCHILL
> (dictating)
> To President Roosevelt. We are
> not going to capitulate. That is
> what the Germans are going to do.

50.   INT.   WHITE HOUSE.   OVAL ROOM

> ROOSEVELT
> Congress require assurances,
> however hypothetical.

51.   INT.   WAR ROOM

CHURCHILL pouring himself immense brandy, and
dictating.

> CHURCHILL
> To give such an assurance would be
> extremely bad for morale here on
> this island at this critical hour.
> But I do so privately, not for
> publication.

52.   INT.   WHITE HOUSE.   OVAL ROOM

ROOSEVELT having breakfast off a tray, dictating.

> ROOSEVELT
> I am trying to help you, as a
> friend ! Private assurances are
> no good. Please make public
> statement.

53.   INT.   CHURCHILL'S BEDROOM

Darkness.

CHURCHILL sits down in dressing gown, brandy glass
in hand, dictating to NIGHT CLERK

> CHURCHILL
> My dear friend, no.

54.   INT. WHITE HOUSE. OVAL ROOM - NIGHT

Just a desk lamp.

                    ROOSEVELT
          Am very worried about this.
          Congress about to vote. Please
          reconsider.

55.   INT. CHURCHILL'S BEDROOM

5 a.m. CHURCHILL in his pyjamas, sitting in an
uncomfortable upright wooden chair.

He is immensely nervous. He knows it is not just
a package of arms, but the whole question of the
will of the American people to get involved in this
war, which is in the balance.

A KNOCK, and ISMAY enters.

                    ISMAY
          Air Marshal Dowding has just
          telephoned, sir. Radar indicates
          the biggest German airstrike yet,
          approaching the coast. He thinks
          it could be the first wave of the
          actual invasion.

CHURCHILL grunts but says nothing.

The TELEPHONE RINGS. ISMAY picks it up.

          Yes ?
                    (listens, then replaces
                    it)
          A telegram is just coming through
          from Washington, sir.

CHURCHILL literally runs from the room.

56.   INT. ANTE ROOM

NIGHT CLERKS manning various communication
equipment.

A teleprinter is thumping out the message with
agonising slowness -

"ROOSEVELT TO FORMER NAVAL PERSON. PLEASE ACCEPT
FROM THE AMERICAN PEOPLE FIFTY DESTROYERS ..."

CHURCHILL throws his arms in the air, and roars
with delight.

57.   INT. WHITE HOUSE. OVAL ROOM

ROOSEVELT dictating. He looks as though he has
had a rough night.

                    ROOSEVELT
          ... packed with various odds and
          ends which you may find useful in
          your little scrap with Mr. Hitler.

58.   ACTUALITY FOOTAGE

The convoy of battleships sailing over the Atlantic.

                    ROOSEVELT (V.O.)
          In return we accept military bases
          in Newfoundland, Bermuda, Bahamas,
          Jamaica, British Guiana ....

A C T   F I V E

59.   INT.   UNDERGROUND.   CORRIDOR

EDEN walking briskly down the corridor to the
War Room. He is tanned and fit.

CHURCHILL greets him most warmly, at the door
to the War Room.

>   CHURCHILL
>   Anthony, Anthony, how relieved
>   I am to see you safely back !

>   EDEN
>   Hallo, Winston.

>   CHURCHILL
>   Five whole weeks of the most
>   terrible risks. Come in, come
>   in, my dear, your friends are
>   most eager to see you ...

60.   INT.   WAR ROOM

>   EDEN
>   Cabinet will have read my telegrams
>   and reports from every stage of my
>   Middle Eastern tour.

>   CHURCHILL
>   An Italian Advance ...

>   EDEN
>   The Italians have advanced fifty
>   miles into Egypt, unopposed. I
>   told you Wavell is planning a
>   defensive battle at Mersah Matra ...

CHURCHILL growls with disgust.

>   However, I have to report something
>   so secret that Wavell begged me not
>   to trust it even to a personal cypher
>   telegram. He wouldn't even tell me,

60.   (CONTINUED)

                              EDEN
                            (cont'd)
              at first. He is planning, not a
              defensive battle at all, but a
              flat-out attack.

CABINET startled and delighted.

                    Now this is deadly secret. There
                    is a tiny gap in the Italians'
                    right flank, in the empty desert.
                              (he shows position on
                              a campaign map which
                              he has marked up)
                    Wavell will make an overnight drive
                    and offensive leap through this
                    gap with his best troops, who will
                    then turn North towards the sea and
                    attack the entire Italian Army from
                    the rear. It is extremely bold and
                    risky. But the prize could be -
                    mass surrenders, and a clear road
                    to drive West towards Tripoli.

General delight from the CABINET.

DILL is clearly shaken that he knows nothing at all
about this.

                              CHURCHILL
                            (eagerly)
                    And when will he attack ?

                              EDEN
              He cannot say.

                              CHURCHILL
              Cannot say ?

                              EDEN
              He's most frightfully sensitive
              about security.

                              CHURCHILL
              But he must tell us !

                              EDEN
              I don't think you'll get it out
              of him, honestly.

                              CHURCHILL
                            (angry now)
              And how long, pray, has he been
              planning this ?

60.   (CONTINUED)

                              EDEN
          I believe some months.

                              CHURCHILL
          Months ?
                              (astounded)
          Then he knew about it when he was
          here, in this room ?

                              DILL
                              (hastily)
          Perhaps Wavell has been influenced
          by the Italian invasion of Greece,
          which was only made possible by a
          leak in Greek security.

                              HALIFAX
          Did Wavell mention that ?

                              EDEN
          No, but the Greek Government
          reminded me most forcibly that we
          have given them specific pledges
          of support, now they are in trouble.

                              ATTLEE
          But we have no troops to give
          support !

                              HALIFAX
          Yes, we have troops.

                              ATTLEE
          Well yes, but none we could
          conceivably spare.

                              HALIFAX
          We gave them our word.

                              CHURCHILL
          You are right, Foreign Secretary.
          If necessary, we will have to
          send them troops from Wavell's
          command.

Hubbub of protest from everyone at the table.

          Greece must not fall. She is the
          very cradle of democracy, which is
          what we are fighting for ! If she
          is crushed, a light will have gone
          out that has illuminated Europe
          for a thousand years !

60.   (CONTINUED)

                         DILL
              But surely you are not going to
              take troops away from Wavell, just
              as he is about to attack ?

                         CHURCHILL
                         (angry)
              About to attack, about to attack,
              how do you know that, pray ?

                         DILL
              Mr. Eden has just said -

                         CHURCHILL
                         (bangs table)
              Can you positively say when he
              will attack ?

                         DILL
              No.

                         CHURCHILL
              Very well ! We have given our
              word to the brave Greeks.
                         (to DILL)
              Telegraph to Wavell demanding to
              know the date of his offensive !

61.   INT.   DESERT H.Q. TENT.   SET UP FOR WAVELL

       WAVELL holds Dill's telegram, and dictates reply.

                         WAVELL
              Wavell to CIGS, for Mr. Churchill.
              Many thanks for your telegram.
              Regret am unable to give the
              information requested. Highest
              degree of secrecy essential.

62.   INT.   WAR ROOM

       CHURCHILL angrily dictating a reply.

       DILL is with him.

62.   (CONTINUED)

                    CHURCHILL
          <u>Demand</u> precise date of intended
          <u>attack</u> ! Whole of Eastern
          Mediterranean position depends on
          it. Kindly cable your troop
          dispositions in full.
                    (to DILL)
          How long would it take me to fly
          out there ?

                    DILL
                    (alarmed)
          Prime Minister, you must leave him
          alone. You must be reasonable
          about this. -

CHURCHILL explodes with wrath.

                    CHURCHILL
          Reasonable, reasonable, you're
          always so damned reasonable,
          you've always got some excuse for
          doing nothing !
                    (savagely)
          Cowardice does not win wars, my
          friend !

63.   <u>NEWSFILM</u>

The Western Desert. Night. Tanks and armoured
cars move stealthily across the sands.

Just the faint creak of their caterpillar tracks
can be heard.

                    WAVELL   (V.O.)
          Wavell to Chief of Imperial
          General Staff, for Mr. Churchill.
          Operation "Compass" moving off
          2 a.m. Request radio blackout,
          for absolute security.

64. INT. CHURCHILL'S BEDROOM

CHURCHILL in bed, with just a low bedside lamp.

He sits up in his green and gold dragon dressing
gown, cigar in mouth, bed littered with papers.

He is reading Wavell's cable.

ISMAY is with him.

                    CHURCHILL
          Agreed. Keep me informed.
          (hands to ISMAY)

The NOISE of an AIR-RAID AND BOMBING can be heard
outside.

CHURCHILL is quiet and thoughtful.

          Do I seem fierce to you ?

                    ISMAY
          Sometimes.

                    CHURCHILL
          I'm gentle as a kitten if I'm
          stroked.

                    ISMAY
          I'll tell that to Dill, shall I ?

CHURCHILL looks at him and grunts.

                    CHURCHILL
          I'll tell him I'm sorry in the
          morning. He knows I'm fierce
          only with one man: Hitler. It
          is regrettable if others sometimes
          get in the way.

The Bombing gets closer.

ISMAY is clearing papers, ashtry, etc.

                    ISMAY
          What will you do when Hitler's dead,
          sir, and the war's over ?

                    CHURCHILL
          Oh, it'll be very dull then. Very
          dull. Now now, Master Winston ...
               (turns over and switches
                off the light)
          ... you can't expect to have a war
               all the time.

65. <u>NEWSFILM</u>

The Blitz.

A hail of bombing onto the City and East End Docks.

66. <u>NEWSFILM</u>

Presidential Elections.

Roosevelt returned with resounding majority.

67. <u>NEWSFILM</u>

Blitz continued - day now, as well as night.

Appalling destruction, London burning.

Sudden tremendous explosion close by.

68. <u>NEWSFILM</u>

Newspaper hordings:

"BUCKINGHAM PALACE: DIRECT HIT"

69. <u>INT. THE KING'S STUDY</u>.

Rubble and wreckage lie everywhere, following
the bombing of the Palace.

The KING and QUEEN are with HALIFAX, still very
shaken and over-excited.

> QUEEN
> My one thought, when I looked
> round at all that destruction,
> was - Thank the Lord, <u>now</u> I can
> look the East End in the face !

> KING
> At least we've still got a roof
> over our heads ! More than some
> of those poor beggars have.

69.   (CONTINUED)

>   HALIFAX
> But there is the greatest concern,
> Ma'am, at the way you and the
> King and Winston immediately
> hurry to the devastated areas -
> sometimes even before the raid
> is over.

>   KING
> Well of course.

>   QUEEN
> Could you stop Winston doing what
> he wants ?

>   KING
> He clambers over the ruins like a
> ten-year old, bulldog jaw set, and
> oh ! - how they love him ! "Give
> it to them, Winnie", they shout,
> "We can take it !" I've seen him
> climb up heaps of rubble that were
> still smouldering, raise his hat
> and stick and cigar in the air,
> and shout "Are we downhearted ?"
> And they all shout "No !"

>   QUEEN
> But I've seen him weep like a child
> over it all, when he thought we
> couldn't see him.

Silence.

>   HALIFAX
> So much depends on him. Could we
> not stop him taking these terrible
> risks ?

70.   INT. CHURCHILL'S BEDROOM

CHURCHILL working up a speech, walking up and down,
acting it out to an imaginary House of Commons.

A SECRETARY takes it down.

>   CHURCHILL
> So do not let us talk of dark days
> - but rather, of glorious days,
> tremendous days, the most glorious
> in our nation's history !
>   (to GIRL)
> Wait. Read that back to me. No.
> Wait. Wait.

70.   (CONTINUED)

CHURCHILL consults his own scribbled notes and tries
a new tack:

> CHURCHILL
> (cont'd)
> These cruel, wanton, indiscriminate
> bombings of London are of course
> part of Hitler's invasion plan. He
> hopes -

ISMAY enters quietly, cable in hand.

> (instantly)
> From Wavell ?

> ISMAY
> No, President Roosevelt. Acknowledging
> your letter saying we had no more
> dollars left to buy arms from him.
> He says he is thinking about it.

CHURCHILL grunts.

> CHURCHILL
> Greece ?

> ISMAY
> Thessalonica and Pireus have both
> fallen.

71.   INT.   WHITE HOUSE.   OVAL ROOM

Roosevelt's famous wireless "Fireside Chats".

He really is at a fireplace (in his wheelchair) with
the microphone set to catch the crackle of the flames
as well.

He is adopting a simple and folksy manner.

> ROOSEVELT
> If Britain should go down, all of
> us in the Americas would be living
> at the point of a Nazi gun. So we
> must produce arms and ships for them
> with every energy and resource we
> can command ... But the British have
> no dollars left. So why don't we
> just lend, or lease, arms to them ?

71.   (CONTINUED)

> ROOSEVELT
> (cont'd)
> Let me put it this way. Suppose
> my neighbour's house catches fire,
> and I have a length of garden hose
> he could put it out with. Do I say,
> "Neighbour, this cost me 15 dollars" ?
> No - I say, "Take it quickly, and let
> me have it back when you've put the
> fire out".
> > (he leans forward to
> > underline his point)
> We in America must become the Arsenal
> of Democracy.

72.   INT. CHURCHILL'S BEDROOM

Darkness.

DILL is shaking CHURCHILL awake, holding a
teleprinter message.

> DILL
> From Wavell.

CHURCHILL grabs it, sits up, holds to light.

> WAVELL (V.O.)
> "Wavell to CIGS. Italians in
> full retreat. 38,000 prisoners
> taken, including four generals ..."

CHURCHILL nearly leaps through the roof with delight.

73.   NEWSFILM

British armour streams full-pelt across the coastal
strip beside the Med.

A heavy barrage of guns clears the way ahead.

> WAVELL (V.O.)
> ... now pushing back remnants of
> Italian invasion force before us.

> CHURCHILL (V.O.)
> Churchill to Wavell. The Army of the
> Nile has rendered glorious service to
> the Empire, reaping rewards in every
> corner ...

74. INT. DESERT H.Q. TENT. SET UP FOR WAVELL

WAVELL sits quietly reading the telegram.

                    CHURCHILL   (V.O.)
          Please cable any requirements.
          See Matthew 7, verse 7 - "Ask,
          and it shall be given you; seek,
          and ye shall find; knock, and it
          shall be opened unto you."

WAVELL to COMMUNICATIONS OFFICER:

                    WAVELL
          Reply - "See St. James I, verse 17".

75. INT. CHURCHILL'S BEDROOM

CHURCHILL pulling on his clothes in great haste.

                    CHURCHILL
          Well, look it up, look it up !

DILL is hastily flicking through the Bible.

He finds the reference.

                    DILL
          "Every good and perfect gift is
          from above, and cometh down from
          the Father of Light ..."

CHURCHILL purrs contentedly.

          " ... with whom there is no
          variableness neither shadow of
          turning."

CHURCHILL does an immense double-take.

76. NEWSFILM

British armour roaring forward to the attack, in
massive force.

77.   INT.   UNDERGROUND ANTE ROOM

CHURCHILL can be heard booming away at a Cabinet
Meeting beyond the doors directly connecting
Ante Room to the War Room.

ISMAY working at his desk, to be on hand if needed.

DILL emerges from the War Room, looking incredulous
and exhausted.

                    DILL
          He's ordering Wavell to halt his
          advance !

ISMAY is astounded.

                    ISMAY
          In favour of Greece ?

                    DILL
               (nods)
          Over 50 percent of his force to
          be transferred.

78.   INT.   DESERT H.Q. TENT.   SET UP FOR WAVELL

WAVELL working at a collapsible card-table,
scribbling the draft of a cable:

                    WAVELL
          Wavell to Prime Minister. Am
          naturally carrying out your orders,
          but am filled with dismay at your
          decision - Intelligence reports
          that German troops and armour
          arrived in Tripoli yesterday, to
          reinforce Italians. Commander, a
          certain General Rommel.

NO SCENE 79.

80.   NEWSFILM

German advance roaring over the desert against
WAVELL.

                    WAVELL (V.O.)
          Wavell to Chief of Imperial General
          Staff, London. Having to retreat in
          face of massive advance by Rommel.

81.   INT.   WAR ROOM

EDEN at his desk.

For once, there is an edge of panic in CHURCHILL's VOICE.

> CHURCHILL
> Tell him to halt at Tobruk, he must turn and make a stand at Tobruk !

> EDEN
> How can he do that ? There is absolutely no strategic reason for halting <u>there</u> ! - The Chiefs of Staff would never agree.

> CHURCHILL
> Then telegraph direct, don't tell the Chiefs of Staff !

> EDEN
> (forcefully)
> Winston, listen, This is the very reason you're facing the Motion of No Confidence in the House - riding roughshod over Wavell and the entire Command, sending his troops to Greece to disaster, against every advice and opinion expressed by -

CHURCHILL grunts, then thrusts a wodge of notes at EDEN.

> What's this ?

> CHURCHILL
> Draft of my speech in defence against the Motion.
> (incredulous)
> No confidence in the way I am running the war ? <u>No confidence</u> ?

> EDEN
> There are a great many people saying openly that your policies are disastrous.

> CHURCHILL
> Jackals and snarling wolves !

He throws himself angrily into a chair, but suddenly speaks quietly:

81.   (CONTINUED)

                              CHURCHILL
                              (cont'd)
                    Only I can win this war. Only I.
                    Not you, not Halifax. Not even the
                    King. I have the steady power of
                    England inside me. I am its strength,
                    its teeth, its ... bite. I must
                    survive, or we will lose.

Pause.

                    Tell Wavell he must halt, then
                    counter-attack.

                              EDEN
                    Then you must give him time to
                    prepare a counter-attack.

CHURCHILL looks at the notes in his hand.

                              CHURCHILL
                    He must do so now.

82.   NEWSFILM

       Operation Battleaxe - the ludicrously premature
       counter attack.

                              WAVELL   (V.O.)
                    Wavell to Chief of Imperial
                    General Staff for Mr. Churchill.
                    Am having to abandon my counter-
                    attack and pull back. Heavy
                    casualties.

83.   INT. CHURCHILL'S BEDROOM

       CHURCHILL sitting alone, drafting telegram in his
       own hand.

                              CHURCHILL   (V.O.)
                    I have come to the conclusion that
                    the public interest will be best
                    served if General Auchinleck relieves
                    you in command of the Middle East.
                    I have greatly admired your conduct,
                    both in success and adversity, but
                    I feel however ....

84.	INT.	DESERT H.Q. TENT SET UP FOR WAVELL

WAVELL quietly reading the telegram.

Silence.

NO SCENE 85

86.	INT.	DESERT H.Q. TENT SET UP FOR WAVELL

WAVELL with his CHIEF OFFICERS, shaking hands and
saying goodbye.

He is dressed for departure.

WAVELL	(V.O.)
Wavell to Prime Minister. I am
sure you are acting wisely.
Auchinleck ideal.

87.	INT.	PLANE.

AUCHINLECK flying out to take command.

He sits reading through briefings and newspapers.

One has the heading - "CHURCHILL - SUBSTANTIAL
MAJORITY IN VOTE OF CENSURE"

ADC
Cairo in an hour, sir.

AUCHINLECK
Thank you.

88.	INT.	DESERT H.Q. TENT

WAVELL about to leave.

He pauses to look round, at the door of tent.

An ADC is packing his personal possessions, framed
photo of wife, etc. carefully in boxes.

The tent looks bare.

A SIGNAL OFFICER comes up with telegram, as he leaves.

89.   INT.   WAVELL'S CAR

    Driving over the desert to the airfield.

    WAVELL opens and reads the telegram.

> CHURCHILL (V.O.)
> Churchill to Wavell, most personal.
> See Malachi Chapter 3 verse 17:
> "And they shall be mine, saith
> the Lord of Hosts, in that day
> when I make up my jewells."

89a.   EXT.   DESERT

    Wavell's car disappearing in long shot, minute in
the vast desert.

    PAN DOWN to the tiny red specks of flowers that he
spoke of, glimmering in the heat haze.

A C T   S I X

90.   NEWSFILM

Operation Barbarossa: the Nazis' colossal and
unexpected onslaught on Russia, 22nd June 1941.

                    CHURCHILL   (V.O.)
          At 4 o'clock this morning, Hitler
          attacked and invaded Russia. So
          now this bloodthirsty guttersnipe
          must launch his mechanised armies
          upon new fields of slaughter,
          pillage and devastation.

          Along a 1500 mile front his armour
          poured into that unsuspecting
          country, while the murderous dive-
          bombing of his Luftwaffe smashed
          the Russian Air Force upon the
          ground.

91.   INT. CHURCHILL'S BEDROOM

BBC microphones set up.

CHURCHILL in the midst of his broadcast.

                    CHURCHILL
          Can you doubt what our policy will
          be ? The Russian danger is our
          danger, and the danger of the United
          States; for the cause of any Russian
          fighting for his hearth and home, is
          the cause of free men in every
          quarter of the globe !

92. <u>NEWSFILM</u>

Barbarossa continued.

> CHURCHILL (V.O.)
> Any man or state who fights against
> Nazism shall have our aid ! We
> shall give whatever help we can
> to Russia, and the Russian peoples !

93. <u>INT. WAR ROOM</u>

The War Cabinet in session.

HALIFAX and CHAMBERLAIN have gone; EDEN, BEAVERBROOK
and ANDERSON are now members.

Cabinet Members are extremely annoyed at Churchill's
broadcast.

> ATTLEE
> You had no right to make such a
> major statement of policy, without
> the specific approval of the War
> Cabinet !

> CHURCHILL
> You disagreed with it ?

> ATTLEE
> That is not the point -

> EDEN
> You may have antagonised the
> Americans, by such unqualified
> commitment to a communist state.

> CHURCHILL
> (bangs table)
> Every single person living on these
> islands agrees with what I said !

> ATTLEE
> I doubt that. I doubt that.

> EDEN
> May I suggest, Prime Minister, that
> it may be more fruitful to pass on
> to Marshall Stalin's response ? He
> demands that we establish a second
> front by an invasion of North West
> Europe immediately, to draw off some
> of the Nazi pressure on <u>his</u> front.

93.   (CONTINUED)

> CHURCHILL
> (dismissive)
> I shall be discussing that whole
> question with President Roosevelt
> when we meet next week. Let us
> stall Mr. Stalin, and pass on to
> General Auchinleck.

> ATTLEE
> But Prime Minister -

> CHURCHILL
> The moment Auchinleck took command,
> I telegraphed him to enquire when
> he proposed to launch his offensive.
> Dill ?

> DILL
> (unhappily)
> He replied - five months at least.

> CHURCHILL
> So I have invited him to London
> for consultations.
> (he glares round
> the table)
> I trust no-one disagrees with that ?

94.   INT. ANTE ROOM

DILL drafting a personal letter in longhand.

> DILL
> ... Should warn you that the
> greatest pressure was brought to
> bear on Wavell to act before he
> was ready. Every commander in
> the field has suffered from great
> and undue Government pressure ...

95.   MIDDLE EASTERN HEADQUARTERS. CAIRO

The Commander in Chief's office: balcony shaded and
cool.

AUCHINLECK standing carefully reading the handwritten letter, about to depart from his plane to
London.

95.   (CONTINUED)

                         DILL   (V.O.)
             .... Wellington suffered from it.
             Haig suffered from it. But you
             must resist it, and hold fast to
             your own judgment, however
             difficult this may be.

96.   INT. CORRIDOR. ANTE ROOM

       CHURCHILL is letting off steam again.

                         DILL   (V.O.)
             I shall do my best to draw off
             the fire. Some, however, is bound
             to get through.

       DILL runs his fingers through his hair. He is pretty
       near the end of his tether.

                    (V.O.) I'm sorry we couldn't get
             you a special plane to come back
             in.

96a.   INT. PLANE

       A bare Dakota from which all seats have been stripped.

       AUCHINLECK trying to sleep on the floor.

       The plane is crammed with OTHER RANKS, trying to sleep.

       One has his foot virtually in AUCHINLECK's ear.

97.   EXT. GROUNDS. CHEQUERS

       A magnificent summer day.

       CHURCHILL walking with AUCHINLECK whose "high,
       dignified and commanding presence" and firm, thoughtful
       manner, are greatly impressive.

       CHURCHILL is trying to imbue him with his own fire-
       eating attitude.

97.   (CONTINUED)

                    CHURCHILL
          You _must_ attack before Rommel.
          You _must_ deny him the initiative !

                    AUCHINLECK
          He won't attack while his supplies
          are being diverted to the Russian
          front.

                    CHURCHILL
          But you're talking of a five-month
          delay !

                    AUCHINLECK
          A five-month _preparation_, Prime
          Minister.

                    CHURCHILL
          For a set-piece battle ?

                    AUCHINLECK
          It's far more than that, sir !
          This is going to be a prolonged
          offensive over vast, empty desert
          - just like a gigantic flat polo
          ground. The action will be swift,
          novel and murderous - the sort of
          thing Rommel's made himself
          brilliant at. Now I have fresh
          troops, tanks, trucks and aircraft
          pouring into my command, and I've
          got to weld that mass of untrained
          material into the 8th Army, to
          fight a desert war utterly unlike
          anything any of us has known before.
          When I've done that, _then_ I'll
          attack.

                    CHURCHILL
          But if you lose the initiative -

                    AUCHINLECK
                    (short)
          I won't.

     Pause.

                    CHURCHILL
                    (abrupt)
          Do you think I was right to sack
          Wavell ?

97.   (CONTINUED)

                         AUCHINLECK
                      (after pause)
          I couldn't say.

                         CHURCHILL
          He was very tired, you know.

                         AUCHINLECK
          He seemed all right to me, sir.

                         CHURCHILL
          Tired in his thinking, it lacked
          dash and boldness. The people in
          this country are tired, General,
          they are brave, yes, but they
          have put up with so much and
          their spirits are starting to flag.
          You see it in their eyes. They
          desperately need a resounding
          victory, something to lift their
          hearts and rouse their blood again !
          That is why you must attack !

                         AUCHINLECK
          If I did, we would be wiped out.

Pause.

They walk.

                         CHURCHILL
                      (suddenly)
          Were you warned that I interfere
          too much ?

                         AUCHINLECK
          Yes.

                         CHURCHILL
          That is because this country chose
          me as its mouthpiece, the embodiment
          of its fighting spirit, which is what
          you serve, General.

                         AUCHINLECK
          Agreed.

                         CHURCHILL
          Humph. You will not lead this new
          Army yourself ?

97.   (CONTINUED)

                         AUCHINLECK
              I've appointed General Cunningham.

      CHURCHILL stops and confronts him angrily.

                         CHURCHILL
              Cunningham ? It is said of you
              that you cannot pick men, General.

                         AUCHINLECK
              Then that's on my head, isn't it
              sir ? You must back me or sack me.

                         CHURCHILL
              I trust it will not come to that.

                         AUCHINLECK
              So do I.

      They look each other in the face.

      CHURCHILL is annoyed that he has not dented
      Auchinleck's apparent imperturbability one jot.

                         CHURCHILL
                         (angrily)
              Surely you can give me something
              I can tell Mr. Roosevelt next
              week ?

                         AUCHINLECK
              Yes, sir.
                         (calmly)
              We attack in five months.

      CHURCHILL bangs his stick on the ground, and
      stumps off towards the house.

98.   INT. WAR ROOM

      ATTLEE working at the Cabinet table, alone.

      He is in Churchill's chair (as Deputy PM) and looks
      tiny in it.

      ISMAY knocks and comes in with telegram.

                         ISMAY
              Prime Minister's acknowledgement
              of the Cabinet's cable at four
              this morning. Roosevelt's agreed
              those points.

98.   (CONTINUED)

ATTLEE ponders the telegram.

                        ATTLEE
          Have you seen Dill this morning ?

                        ISMAY
          No ?

                        ATTLEE
          Needs a doctor; he's cracking up.

                        ISMAY
          It's hardly surprising. For
          twelve months, he's suffered a
          daily sixteen hour sledgehammering
          from Winston, and then had to go
          home exhausted to his sick wife.

                        ATTLEE
          I didn't know she was sick.

                        ISMAY
          She was paralysed during the Blitz.
          He doesn't talk about it, but
          apparently she struggles to make
          herself understood, but can't
          speak properly. He has no-one
          to unburden himself to, because
          she can't follow what he's saying.

                        ATTLEE
          Dear God.

                        ISMAY
          I'm sure Winston doesn't know.

                        ATTLEE
          It's him I'm worried about.

                        ISMAY
          Winston ?

                        ATTLEE
          How long can he stand the strain ?
          At sixty-seven, there must be a
          limit. I look at him in Cabinet
          sometimes and think - half the
          world's bearing down on that head.

99.   INT. ANTE ROOM

The Ante Room has been re-arranged as a temporary
dining room.

Those present are in mess jackets or their own form
of dinner dress.

It is after dinner, and the ladies have left.

Present now are CHURCHILL, DILL, BROOKE, ISMAY,
EDEN, POUND and other nonspeaking SENIOR OFFICERS.

CHURCHILL is in the middle of describing the Cavalry
charge at Omdurman in 1899, in which he took part.

He is in terrific form.

                    CHURCHILL
          ... We trotted in columns of troops
          across their left front, then right
          wheel, and charge ! While the
          trumpet was still jerking, we were
          at full gallop towards them, sabres
          high in the air ! I drew my Mauser
          pistol, and cocked it. I could see
          the Dervish riflemen blazing straight
          at us, twelve deep.

          I shouted to my left troop leader to
          shoulder, and we actually crashed
          into the enemy line in crescent
          formation. One man fell beside me -
          instantly cut to pieces. I fired
          right into their faces - left and
          right, swinging my horse's head,
          striking with my pistol butt - killed
          three for certain, two doubtful -
          and cleared their line. Then I saw
          two dervishes on their knees taking
          aim with rifles - and for the first
          time the danger and peril of it all
          came home to me. I wheeled round and
          galloped straight at them, riding
          them down, and their bullets whizzed
          past my ear.

          As I got back to base, the wounded
          started to come in, in that broiling
          sun. Horses spouting blood,
          struggling on three legs, men
          staggering on foot, bleeding from
          terrible wounds, fishhook spears
          stuck right through them, men
          gasping, crying, collapsing, expiring.

99.   (CONTINUED)

Silence.

                         CHURCHILL
                         (cont.)
          Yet out of three hundred and ten
          officers and men, we lost only
          twenty-one - against the most
          terrible odds which should have
          meant annihilation for all of us ...
                    (from the bottom of
                    his soul)
          ... Because of the resolution and
          determination with which we went
          into that battle !!

CHURCHILL sits back and drinks.

Silence for a while.

                         BROOKE
                         (quietly)
          But there is all the difference
          in the world between the cavalry
          charge at Omdurman in 1899, and
          modern warfare.

                         CHURCHILL
                         (pouncing)
          But there is no difference in
          men's spirits; it is in their
          hearts that battles are won !
          Witness Auchinleck - Auchinleck
          has made a most sluggish start to
          his advance; already he has had
          to replace his 8th Army commander
          for funking it.

                         EDEN
          It is caution, not sluggishness.

                         BROOKE
          Rommel always advances most
          cautiously.

                         CHURCHILL
          And this new General Ritchie he has
          put in command, who is he ? His
          own chief of staff, with no
          experience of battle whatever !
          Little minds, they all have little
          minds.
                    (suddenly red in the
                    face)
          If Auchinleck loses Egypt, blood
          will flow ! I shall have firing
          parties to shoot the Generals !

99.   (CONTINUED)

An icy silence.

CHURCHILL for once realises that he has overstepped
the mark, he feels the hostility all around the table.

He abruptly laughs, and starts to sing, waving his
cigar to the tune:

                    CHURCHILL
                    (cont'd)
         "I went in to pay the bill
         But instead I took the till,
         My wife and kids were starving".

DILL rises.

                    DILL
         If you will excuse me for a
         moment, sir, I must telephone to
         my wife.

                    CHURCHILL
                  (waves cigar)
         Of course, of course.

The moment Dill has left, CHURCHILL beckons to BROOKE.

         Come over here, Brooke, I want to
         talk to you.

He and BROOKE retire to a corner with the port
decanter.

         You saw Dill just then ? The
         way he went out ?

                    BROOKE
         Yes, sir ?

                    CHURCHILL
         I have made up my mind to relieve
         him, and I should like you to take
         over as Chief of Imperial General
         Staff.

BROOKE's head spins.

         What's the matter ?

                    BROOKE
         I am astounded, sir.

99.   (CONTINUED)

                    CHURCHILL
          Why ? Do you not think we could
          work together ?

                    BROOKE
          It won't be a bed of roses, but I -

                    CHURCHILL
                    (wide-eyed)
          Why should it not be ? I am the
          most amenable fellow, if spoken to
          nicely. And you always tell me the
          truth, without trying to bully me
          about it, or tell me to be
          reasonable. I'm not reasonable,
          never will be. Also Dill is an
          exhausted man.

                    BROOKE
          Because it's his job to stop you
          squandering what little resources
          we have.

                    CHURCHILL
                    (growl)
          He's always saying "no".

                    BROOKE
          I shall say no sometimes.

                    CHURCHILL
          I don't mind argument, so long
          as I win. You will accept ?

Pause.

                    BROOKE
          Of course.

CHURCHILL takes his hand impulsively.

                    CHURCHILL
          Thank you, thank you, my dear !
          And always remember this -
                    (suddenly vehement)
          I am a man in a rage to win this
          war, to defend the country I love
          and to shatter the evil of Nazism.
          Together, I am convinced we could
          do just that.

99.   (CONTINUED)

Churchill's BUTLER comes up.

                    BUTLER
          Excuse me, sir.

                    CHURCHILL
          Yes, yes, what is it ?

                    BUTLER
          We've just heard it on the
          midnight news, sir. The
          Japanese have attacked the
          Americans.

                    CHURCHILL
          Bosh.

                    BUTLER
          It was on the BBC, sir.

CHURCHILL lurches up and back to his seat at the
table.

                    CHURCHILL
          I would have heard about it
          from the Cabinet Office.

                    BROOKE
          What exactly did they say ?

                    BUTLER
          Just that the Japanese airforce
          had attacked the American Fleet
          at Hawaii.

The conversation has stopped round the room:

Everyone is listening now.

CHURCHILL pulls himself upright, and strides from
the room.

100. <u>INT. CHURCHILL'S BEDROOM</u>

CHURCHILL on telephone.

       CHURCHILL
   Mr. President ?

       ROOSEVELT
      (distort)
   It's quite true. They attacked
   us at Pearl Harbour. They're also
   attacking Hong Kong, Siam and
   Malaya. We're all in the same
   boat, now.

ON CHURCHILL.

A C T   S E V E N

101. INT. UNDERGROUND CORRIDOR

SIR CHARLES WILSON, Churchill's doctor, hurries
down the long corridor towards the Ante Room.

He is sixty, rather wizened, sharp, direct, self-
seeking.

There is great bustling activity and moving of
desks and files:

Churchill's decision to rush to America immediately
means a major upheaval of the Cabinet Secretariat
by lunchtime.

102. INT. ANTE ROOM

EDEN waylays WILSON as he enters.

                    EDEN
          Sir Charles.

                    WILSON
          I've been called in to see the
          Prime Minister.

                    EDEN
          He's just walking round from the
          House of Commons.

                    WILSON
          Walking ? But there's an air-
          raid going on !

                    EDEN
          That just adds to the fun as far
          as he's concerned. In any case,
          I called you.

                    WILSON
          Indeed ?

102. (CONTINUED)

                    EDEN
          We're getting seriously worried about
          his health - the strain he's under
          is simply colossal. You know he's
          dashing off to Washington tonight ?

                    WILSON
          Exactly why are you worried ?

103. EXT. HORSEGUARDS - DAY   O/B

CHURCHILL striding along at tremendous pace, swinging
his gold-topped cane.

CHURCHILL is as buoyant and excited as he was in
May 1940.

BROOKE is having to work hard to keep up with him.

                    CHURCHILL
          You can mind the shop while
          I'm away. Attlee will assist
          you, as deputy PM. Don't take
          any nonsense from him - he's
          just a sheep in sheep's clothing.

                    BROOKE
          You need to take a military adviser
          to Washington. If I can't go, it
          should be Dill.

                    CHURCHILL
          Well, perhaps.

                    BROOKE
          As C.I.G.S., I must insist.

                    CHURCHILL
                 (growl)
          Really ?

                    BROOKE
          I should also tell you, sir, that
          I'm preparing a paper for the
          War Cabinet strongly opposing
          your wish to send five hundred
          tanks to help the Russians.

CHURCHILL stops in his tracks.

103.   (CONTINUED)

                              CHURCHILL
                    Are you now !

                              BROOKE
                    If the Red Army collapses, the
                    invasion of Britain would follow,
                    and tank battles would be fought
                    on British soil similar to those
                    being fought in the Western Desert.

CHURCHILL strides on again.

                    We must not squander our resources,
                    I would not accept that ...

CHURCHILL's eyebrows are going up. Now BROOKE is
in the saddle, he is coming on far stronger than
anticipated.

103a.   INT.   UNDERGROUND CORRIDOR

They are striding down the corridor.

                              BROOKE
                    And to be frank, Prime Minister,
                    I'm appalled to discover a total
                    lack of overall policy for the
                    prosecution of the war.

                              CHURCHILL
                              (growl)
                    You've never said this before.

                              BROOKE
                    I've never been C.I.G.S. before.
                    We work from day to day, from
                    hand to mouth ... Improvisation
                    is all very well, but appallingly
                    wasteful of effort and resources ...

Enters the Ante Room.

104.   INT.   ANTE ROOM

CHURCHILL spots WILSON as he enters.

                              CHURCHILL
                              (snap)
                    What do you want ?

104. (CONTINUED)

                    WILSON
          I hear you're off to America.

                    CHURCHILL
          What of it, what of it ?

                    WILSON
          Then I should check you over.

                    CHURCHILL
                    (angry)
          There's absolutely nothing wrong
          with me ! Fuss fuss fuss ...

He bangs the doors to the War Room open, and enters,
followed by the other two.

105. INT. WAR ROOM

As they enter.

                    CHURCHILL
          Dispepsia is my only complaint,
          and the cure for that is breathing
          exercises.

CHURCHILL flips through telegrams and papers waiting
for him on his table, as WILSON tries to take his
pulse, look in his eyes, etc.

                    WILSON
          You're going by boat ?

                    CHURCHILL
          By battleship.

                    WILSON
          As long as you're not flying.

                    CHURCHILL
          If I want to fly, I'd fly !

                    WILSON
          Tongue ?

                    CHURCHILL
          Aaaagh.

                    WILSON
          You're eating alright ?

105. (CONTINUED)

                         CHURCHILL
          Like a horse.

                         WILSON
          Sleeping ?

                         CHURCHILL
          Like a top.

                         WILSON
          How do you manage that, with
          all the worries you have ?

                         CHURCHILL
          I put my head on the pillow, say
          damn everybody, and go out like
          a light.
                    (to BROOKE)
          It has been impossible to form a
          master plan, because so far we
          have been living from crisis to
          crisis.

                         BROOKE
          That's only partly true, sir,
          it's how you like to see it.

CHURCHILL rounds on him, astonished.

          With the Americans in, we can
          surely arrive at a coherent
          strategy now.

WILSON has finished.

                         CHURCHILL
                    (snap)
          Well ?

                         WILSON
          You're overdoing it.

                         CHURCHILL
          Nonsense.

                         WILSON
          At any rate, I should come
          with you.

                         CHURCHILL
          Alright, alright.
                    (to BROOKE)
          I suppose you imagine you're
          trying to discover a method of
          working with me ?

105. (CONTINUED)

                         BROOKE
            Among other things.

                         CHURCHILL
            Well, I'll tell you what I want
            from a C.I.G.S. Reasonable
            discussion on any topic ....
                    (going out to Ante
                    Room and waving
                    telegram)
            ... followed by complete agree-
            ment with whatever it was I said
            in the first place.

106. NEWSFILM

      Aerial view of the 'Duke of York' and attendant
      flotilla of guardian battle-ships, steaming across
      the U-boat infested waters of the Atlantic.

      Shots of a U-boat sighting and depth charge attack.

      CONGREGATION HEARD singing OVER:

                         CONGREGATION
                         (singing)
                "The first Noel the Angel did say
                Was to certain poor shepherds in fields
                Where they lay ..."

107. INT. OVAL ROOM. WHITE HOUSE

      A small dining table for ROOSEVELT, CHURCHILL and
      HOPKINS.

      The room is decorated for Christmas with a tree,
      streamers, cards, holly, etc.

      ROOSEVELT is serving with the help of a BLACK SERVANT.

      He still shakes with emotion as he tells the story:

107. (CONTINUED)

                    ROOSEVELT
          There were ninety-four ships of
          the American Navy in Pearl Harbour,
          Mr. Churchill. As it was a Sunday,
          there was nothing much happening.
          A lovely sunny day. Some of the
          men were swimming, some getting
          ready for church. They had no
          warning whatsoever. Pass Mr.
          Churchill the potatoes, will you ?
          The first bomb fell at five minutes
          to eight, then 360 Jap aircraft
          came over, just bombing and
          strafing unmercifully. The
          Arizona blew up, the Oklahoma
          capsized, the West Virginia and
          California sunk at their moorings
          .... over 2,000 of our boys killed,
          and 2,000 most terribly wounded.
          I've seen photographs of the way
          those poor boys were burned !

                    HOPKINS
          The shock to the American people
          has been profound, you know.

                    CHURCHILL
          Of course, of course. I know that
          has been burning in my mind ever
          since I heard of that terrible
          morning ...

                    ROOSEVELT
          Please, go ahead.

                    CHURCHILL
                 (earnestly)
          Will this mean that you will have
          to turn your main war effort against
          the Japanese first ?

                    ROOSEVELT
          Oh no, no question of that !

                    CHURCHILL
          Ah !

                    HOPKINS
          Germans first, Japs second, isn't
          that what you said, Mr. President ?

                    CHURCHILL
          I should like to refer to that in
          my speech to Congress.

107.   (CONTINUED)

> ROOSEVELT
> I believe General George Marshall
> the Chief of Staff and the
> Secretary of War Mr. Stimson are
> thrashing out the details with
> your Chiefs of Staff right now.
> Try some cranberry sauce with that,
> it's very good. You see, I think
> we should divide the world into
> maybe three different theatres of
> war. We'll take the Pacific; you
> take the Middle East and Indian
> Ocean; you need some more gravy
> with that, give him some more gravy,
> will you ? And we should combine
> over Europe and the Atlantic Ocean.

> CHURCHILL
> Each nation providing for its own
> theatres, alone ?

> ROOSEVELT
> Oh no ! We'll pool everything.

CHURCHILL delighted.

108.   INT.   WHITE HOUSE.   SMALL PLAIN OFFICE

MARSHALL, DILL, STIMSON, ISMAY round a table. With them,
other nonspeaking SENIOR OFFICERS.

GENERAL GEORGE MARSHALL, now sixty-one, is Chief of
Army General Staff (i.e. Brooke's counterpart). He is
a man of unshaken integrity: he speaks and carries
himself with great dignity, and is at first meeting,
rather cold and aloof.

STIMSON, the U.S. Secretary of War, is now seventy-two.

He is of old aristocratic stock, rather lofty in manner.

> MARSHALL
> One. We propose that the war
> should be run from now on by a
> Joint Chiefs of Staff Committee.
> Just like yours in London, but
> sitting with your American
> counterparts.

> DILL
> In London.

108. (CONTINUED)

                    STIMSON
No, here.

                    DILL
So direction of the war would pass
to Washington ?

                    STIMSON
Yes, sir.

                    MARSHALL
Two. We have considered the
British idea for a joint landing
in Morocco and Algeria to move
East and join up with a victorious
8th Army moving West, thus clearing
North Africa of the enemy
completely.

                    DILL
That's putting it very simply,
General Marshall.

                    MARSHALL
                (politely)
I always try to discuss big issues
in simple form, General Dill. We
have nothing against this plan.

                    ISMAY
You endorse it ?

                    STIMSON
                (shrug)
We have nothing against it.

                    MARSHALL
It'll be fairly soon, we imagine.

                    STIMSON
But it would be no more than
"nibbling at the edges". What
we need is a massive frontal assault
on the coast of France, to drive
straight through to Berlin. We
could get down to that, once this
North African party is out of the
way.

                    ISMAY
The timing is dependent on a
victorious 8th Army advancing West,
Mr. Stimson.

108. (CONTINUED)

> MARSHALL
> Forgive me, but they're not
> exactly victorious just yet, sir.

> ISMAY
> (wry)
> Correct.

> STIMSON
> Perhaps Prime Minister Churchill
> could give your General Auchinleck
> a little nudge about that ?

ISMAY and DILL exchange deadpan glances.

> ISMAY
> Could we persuade him to give
> Auchinleck a little nudge, do you
> think ?

> DILL
> We could always try.

109a. <u>INT. BEDROOM. WHITE HOUSE - NIGHT</u>

Just a side-lamp or two. A fire in the grate.

CHURCHILL in braces and shirtsleeves is rehearsing
his speech to Congress, from typed notes. He is alone,
and gives a terrific performance.

> CHURCHILL
> What sort of people do they think
> we are ?! Is it possible the
> Japanese do not realise that we
> shall never cease to persevere
> until they have been taught a
> lesson which they and the world
> will never forget ?

He stops, consults his notes, and takes the last phrase
again, slightly differently -

> ... which they and the world will
> never forget ?

He swigs brandy and soda while finding another place,
flipping over notes, and tries it out, tasting the
phrases -

109a. (CONTINUED)

                    CHURCHILL
                    (cont'd)
          It is a fact that the British
          Empire, which many thought
          eighteen months ago was broken
          and ruined, is now incomparably
          stronger each month ! But the
          best tidings of all is that the
          United States, united as never
          before, have drawn the sword for
          freedom, and cast away the
          scabbard !

He reaches this climax in a fine fury, and pauses to
make some manuscript alterations.

He abruptly feels hot and rather faint, and crosses
to open the window. He gives a sudden lurch and
staggers. There is a pain above his heart, and he
is breathless.

Frightened, he manages to get to the telephone and
lift it.

109b. INT. BEDROOM. WHITE HOUSE. LATER

WILSON examining him in silence.

CHURCHILL lies out on a couch.

                    CHURCHILL
          Is it my heart ?

WILSON removes his stethoscope, and sits to think.

          A ... a heart attack ?

                    WILSON
          The papers would call it that.

                    CHURCHILL
          What is the treatment ?

                    WILSON
          Six weeks doing nothing.

                    CHURCHILL
          Impossible ! Not now ! With
          America just in the war !

109b. (CONTINUED)

>   WILSON
>   Well, let's say you've been
>   overdoing it. Circulation a
>   bit sluggish.

>   CHURCHILL
>   What does that mean ?

>   WILSON
>   You must give up cigars and that
>   filthy snuff.

>   CHURCHILL
>   My God, it's serious.

>   WILSON
>   Come on, I'll get you to bed.

CHURCHILL is quite frightened.

WILSON helps him up.

CHURCHILL keeps hold of him.

>   CHURCHILL
>   I'd like you to come with me from
>   now on, Charles. Fly back in the
>   plane with me. You must look
>   after me.

>   WILSON
>   Then you must promise to obey my
>   instructions.

>   CHURCHILL
>   Of course, of course.

They start to go.

>   Provided I don't find them
>   disagreeable ....

110. <u>NEWSFILM</u>

Dawn, the desert.

German motorised infantry creeping forward cautiously
in the first light.

110.   (CONTINUED)

                                    AUCHINLECK   (V.O.)
                          Auchinleck to Prime Minister.
                          German reconnaissance force of
                          three columns penetrated gap in
                          our contact troops this morning.
                          Forced to withdraw to Agedabia
                          to reform.

111.   INT.   FLYING BOAT

        CHURCHILL drafting a reply and handing it to an A.D.C.

                                    CHURCHILL   (V.O.)
                          Churchill to Auchinleck. Deeply
                          disturbed to hear of Rommel pre-
                          empting your offensive. Pray
                          advise me of your plans to counter-
                          attack.

112.   EXT.   MIDDLE EAST COMMAND H.Q. CAIRO

        AUCHINLECK working; in front of him are battle reports
        and maps.

                                    AUCHINLECK
                                 (dictating)
                          I realise the public at home may
                          be upset by enemy reoccupation
                          Agedabia, but suspect Rommel over-
                          reaching himself. Our line reforming
                          Sauno-Benghazi, which has not been
                          evacuated yet.

113.   INT.   UNDERGROUND CORRIDOR.

        CHURCHILL arriving back, still in hat and coat, striding
        down the long corridor, followed by BROOKE and
        SECRETARIES.

        Resident STAFF greet him, but his face is black with
        annoyance.

113. (CONTINUED)

>   CHURCHILL   (V.O.)
> Benghazi not evacuated "yet" ?
> Pray telegraph explanation. Have
> you suffered unreported defeat ?
> If losses continue, insist that
> you personally take over command
> of 8th Army from Ritchie.

114. INT. DESERT H.Q. TENT SET UP FOR AUCHINLECK

AUCHINLECK with RITCHIE, at his desk. They refer to
maps.

It is tremendously hot.

>   AUCHINLECK
>   (dictating)
> Have flown today to 8th Army H.Q.,
> am now with Ritchie. I was compelled
> to evacuate Benghazi temporarily, due
> to Rommel's lightening advance.
> Pulling back today to new line
> Tobruk/Agazala.

115. INT. WAR ROOM - NIGHT

BROOKE and ISMAY pouring over desert maps on Cabinet
table:

CHURCHILL in foreground, dictating, dismayed and angry.

>   CHURCHILL
>   (dictating)
> Deeply distressed loss of Benghazi
> with no report of your attempt to
> defend it ! Tobruk/Gazala line
> represents retreat of 300 miles
> in one week ! Pray advise me
> immediately proposed dates of
> counter-attack !

116. <u>INT. DESERT H.Q. TENT SET UP FOR AUCHINLECK</u>

A Conference in progress between AUCHINLECK, RITCHIE
and other SENIOR OFFICERS.

> AUCHINLECK (V.O.)
> Proposed hold present position for
> four months to prepare counter-
> attack.

117. <u>INT. WAR ROOM</u>

War Cabinet in session - CHURCHILL obviously furious
at Auchinleck's answer, haranguing Cabinet:

> CHURCHILL (V.O.)
> Four months delay totally
> unacceptable. I should be glad
> if you will come to London for
> immediate consultations !

118. <u>NEWSFILM</u>

LONG SHOT 8th Army H.Q. half-hidden in the sand-dunes;
a few caravans and tents and lorries, looking bleak and
lonely in the desert. Sand is blown about.

> AUCHINLECK (V.O.)
> Auchinleck to Churchill. Cannot
> leave here at present. Can give no
> more information in person than can
> be given by cable.

119. <u>INT. CHURCHILL'S BEDROOM</u>

CHURCHILL in bed, propped up on the pillows in his
green and gold oriental dressing gown, hair ruffled up,
cigar in mouth, bed littered with cigar ash, newspapers,
dispatches, half-finished breakfast tray.

BROOKE is immaculate in neat uniform.

119.   (CONTINUED)

                    CHURCHILL
                      (shout)
Too busy to talk to us ? Too
busy ?!

                    BROOKE
He has no time to return home,
simply for a Churchillian
browbeating.

                    CHURCHILL
Then I shall go to him.

                    BROOKE
No, sir !

                    CHURCHILL
But the bloody man is holding
up the entire war ! We've got
to get North Africa out of the
way before we can start on
Northern France !

                    BROOKE
Your place is here, sir. I can
go out to Egypt.

                    CHURCHILL
Ha !

                    BROOKE
You would receive an entirely
dispassionate report -

                    CHURCHILL
I wouldn't want one. Dispassionate ?
I have no time for anyone not
thoroughly partisan and bigoted.
I'll go and see Auchinleck. You
stay here and run the rest of the
war. We must produce some action,
or I shall lose control of the
whole scene.
                      (he wriggles and frets
                       like a frustrated
                       little child)
Where can we do something now ?
What about Norway ?

                    BROOKE
                      (almost yelping)
No, sir !

119.   (CONTINUED)

                              CHURCHILL
                              (eagerly)
          We've often discussed another
          Norwegian invasion.

                              BROOKE
          It's an entirely fantastic project,
          sir, doomed from the start.

                              CHURCHILL
          Aden, then, or the Balkans. We
          must be able to do something.
                              (suddenly)
          Why don't you take over the Middle
          East command from Auchinleck ?

                              BROOKE
          Certainly not.

                              CHURCHILL
                              (glare)
          Well, I'm going to Egypt; you're
          staying here.

120.   EXT.   WHITEHALL   (O.B.)

          ISMAY and BROOKE, walking briskly out of Admiralty House
          (salutes from SENTRIES) and turning into Whitehall.

                              BROOKE
          I must go with him. It would be
          absolutely disastrous if he
          started running around the
          battlefield, unchecked. I
          wouldn't put it past him to sack
          Auchinleck and take over the 8th
          Army himself. Probably on horse-
          back, waving a sword.

                              ISMAY
          He's got to do something dramatic,
          if he's to survive the vote of
          censure.

                              BROOKE
          The what ?

                              ISMAY
          You didn't know ? "This House has
          no confidence in the central
          direction of the War." A lot of
          people think that this time, he
          won't survive.

121. INT. OVAL ROOM. WHITE HOUSE

ROOSEVELT is reading through an operational plan in
a red folder.

Starting on CLOSE SHOT of him and PULLING OUT, we can
see his steely calculation as he reads - an aspect of
his character always carefully hidden behind bonhomie
when with others.

ROOSEVELT finishes and, after reflection, presses an
intercom.

                    ROOSEVELT
          Right.

MARSHALL and STIMSON enter as ROOSEVELT wheels himself
to desk.

          Come in, gentlemen. As an
          operational plan, it's most
          impressive. But we did agree
          that we'd clear up North Africa
          before we -
                    (he taps folder)
          - launch the invasion of Northern
          France.

                    STIMSON
          At the rate the British are going,
          they'll never clear North Africa,
          sir.

                    ROOSEVELT
          Hmm. Who drew this up ?

                    MARSHALL
          Major-General Eisenhower, sir.

                    ROOSEVELT
          He's that new Head of ... Army
          Planning and Operations ? Didn't
          you pick him, George ?

                    MARSHALL
          Yes, sir.

                    STIMSON
          One thing concerns me, sir. That
                    (points)
          would clearly mean this war is no
          longer a one-man show.

121. (CONTINUED)

>   ROOSEVELT
>   (after thought)
>   Maybe that's happening anyhow.
>   (taps the file)
>   Tell Eisenhower to start
>   detailed planning.

122. <u>INT. CHURCHILL'S BEDROOM</u>

WILSON is examining CHURCHILL.

BROOKE present.

>   WILSON
>   You're flying this time.

>   CHURCHILL
>   (nods)
>   In a converted Liberator.   No
>   seating, no heating.

>   WILSON
>   You're mad.
>   (straightens)
>   I'm coming with you.

>   CHURCHILL
>   (soothed)
>   Good, good.

>   BROOKE
>   Do you know, sir, I've never
>   seen the Nile ? There are five
>   different sorts of heron who
>   live on it, which live nowhere
>   else in the world. I should so
>   like to see them.

CHURCHILL's eyes instantly fill with moisture.

He holds BROOKE's shoulders, very sentimental.

>   CHURCHILL
>   Then of course you must come too,
>   my dear.
>   (turns away)
>   You may well have a new Prime
>   Minister by the time we leave,
>   anyhow.

123. <u>STILLS: EXT. HOUSE OF COMMONS</u>

STILLS of the House sandbagged and barricaded.

The House can be HEARD OVER, noisy and distracted.
Some Members vituperate Churchill, others shout in
defence of him.

OVER C.U. CHURCHILL:

> MEMBER (V.O.)
> For close on three years, we
> have had an almost unbroken record
> of defeats, all over the world.
> And no-one dares put the blame
> where it belongs - on the Prime
> Minister !

Roars of disagreement.

> We never had anything in the last
> war comparable with <u>this</u> series
> of disasters !

Applause and noisy comment.

> 2nd MEMBER
> This motion is not an attack on
> officers in the field, but upon
> the central direction here in
> London ! The cause of our failure
> sits there !

He points to CHURCHILL.

> 3rd MEMBER
> Not only Cairo and Alexandria, but
> the Suez Canal and all the oilfields
> of the Middle East are at the mercy
> of Rommel ! This is the eleventh
> hour, the last chance; are we going
> to throw it away ?

Roars of No !

<u>(INTERVAL)</u>

A C T E I G H T

125. <u>NEWSFILM</u>

A Liberator flying high up and alone, over the
Mediterranean. No escort planes.

125a. <u>INT. PLANE</u>

CHURCHILL, WILSON, BROOKE and SECRETARIES sit or lie
huddled in blankets on the metal floor of the bomb-
racks.

CHURCHILL is staring moodily from a tiny observation
port.

        CHURCHILL
  My last chance, Charles.

        WILSON
  You had a good enough majority !

        CHURCHILL
  I'm so tired.

125b. <u>NEWSFILM</u>

8th Army field H.Q.

A desolate scene amidst sand-dunes, a few trucks,
one caravan, no tents. Work is being done in the
open air, or in the back of trucks.

It is colossally hot, and the place is alive with
flies.

The desert wind blows continuously.

126. EXT. "THE CAGE"

A wire mosquito net erected around and above a
table in the open air.

The flies of Egypt seem to live inside, unable to
get out. The heat is broiling.

CHURCHILL and AUCHINLECK eating together, continually
waving flies off their food.

AUCHINLECK is explaining a point (mute). CHURCHILL
is not so much listening, as looking at his eyes -
they are tired and dull. The desert wind blows.

127. H.Q. MIDDLE EAST COMMAND. THE C-IN-C's ROOM

BROOKE with CHURCHILL, who is going through a
handwritten list with savage relish.

                    CHURCHILL
          Auchinleck to go as Commander-
          in-Chief and be replaced by
          Alexander, from Burma.
          Auchinleck to go as commander
          of the 8th Army, and be replaced
          by General Gott.

                    BROOKE
          Gott !

                    CHURCHILL
          General Ramsden to be sacked,
          General Dorman-Smith to be
          sacked, General Corbett to be
          sacked -

                    BROOKE
               (horrified)
          No, no, sir, you can't do that !

                    CHURCHILL
          Why cannot I do that, pray ?

                    BROOKE
          You must not dismiss senior
          officers merely for acting under
          orders ! And Gott, Gott for the
          8th Army !

127. (CONTINUED)

                              CHURCHILL
                    What is wrong with Gott, pray ?

                              BROOKE
                    He's been out here for years,
                    he's exhausted. If you must
                    have a massacre of Generals,
                    bring in some fresh blood.

                              CHURCHILL
                    Who ?

                              BROOKE
                         (after thought)
                    Montgomery.

                              CHURCHILL
                    Nonsense.

                              BROOKE
                    No, sir.

                              CHURCHILL
                    He has no experience of desert
                    warfare at all !

                              BROOKE
                    Well, certainly not Gott !

CHURCHILL glowers at him, then slams angrily out of
the door to his adjacent bedroom.

128.   H.Q. MIDDLE EAST COMMAND. THE C-IN-C's ROOM.
       THE SAME NIGHT

BROOKE asleep in a low camp-bed.

Darkness.

CHURCHILL suddenly bursts in, in his pyjamas.

                              CHURCHILL
                    Brookie, Brookie ! We'll split
                    the Middle East command into two:
                    Near East, and Persia-Iraq. You
                    take over as C-in-C   Near East,
                    with Monty under you as 8th Army
                    Commander and we'll offer Persia-
                    Iraq to Auchinleck.

128. (CONTINUED)

> BROOKE
> What ?

> CHURCHILL
> Well, we ought to give him
> something. He's a noble fellow.
> Perhaps I'm being a bit hard on
> him.

> BROOKE
> (sitting up)
> It's an attractive idea.

> CHURCHILL
> Ah-ha, my dear fellow, I know
> how you pine for a command again ...

> BROOKE
> But who would keep you under control,
> sir ?

> CHURCHILL
> "Under control" ?

> BROOKE
> (after thought)
> I'm grateful, sir, but no. My place
> is with you.

> CHURCHILL
> Humph. That leaves us with
> Alexander, then.

The TELEPHONE BUZZES. He takes it.

> Prime Minister. No, he's here.
> Well tell me, he's in bed.
> (he listens)
> I see. When was this ?
> (he listens, then
> gravely replaces
> the receiver)
> General Gott was shot down and
> killed at ten last night. Flying
> exactly the same route we flew to
> get here.

Silence.

> BROOKE
> Monty, then.

128. (CONTINUED)

                         CHURCHILL
                          (nods)
             Under Alexander.

                         BROOKE
             A good team.

                         CHURCHILL
                          (grunts. then:)
             Cable them, will you ? They
             must come now.

129. INT. UNDERGROUND ANTE ROOM

    ISMAY is with MONTGOMERY, who is just dashing for
    the airport.

    Briefcases, overnight bags, etc. are in evidence.

    ISMAY hands over a thick file.

                         ISMAY
             That's all the briefing I could
             get together at such notice.
                          (hands file)
             It must have been quite a shock.

                         MONTGOMERY
             I wasn't shocked. I was thinking,
             how extraordinary it is. A soldier
             gives his whole life to his
             profession, with no reward for
             years. Then suddenly, fortune
             smiles, there comes a gleam of
             success, he gains advancement,
             opportunity presents itself, he
             gets a great command. He wins a
             victory, becomes world-famous,
             even. Then his luck changes. At
             one stroke all his life's work
             flashes away - perhaps through no
             fault of his own - and he is flung
             into the endless catalogue of
             military failures.

    Crosses to leave.

129. (CONTINUED)

> ISMAY
> Oh come, you oughtn't to take
> it like that. I don't think
> you're going to disaster.

MONTGOMERY spins round as if shot.

> MONTGOMERY
> What ? What do you mean ? I
> was talking about Wommle !

130. H.Q. MIDDLE EAST COMMAND. THE C-IN-C's ROOM

CHURCHILL sits slumped in an armchair, deeply
depressed.

BROOKE stands by him, reporting.

> BROOKE
> Sir Ian Jacob took your letter
> of dismissal to Auchinleck in
> person, sir. He drove out and
> gave it to him in the Map caravan
> of the 8th Army H.Q. He said
> he felt as if he was going to
> murder an old friend.

> CHURCHILL
> (grave)
> It was like killing a magnificent
> stag.

Silence.

An ORDERLY knocks and comes in.

> ORDERLY
> Excuse me, sir - General
> Alexander's car has just arrived
> from the airport.

> CHURCHILL
> (roar)
> Alex ! Alex, come in !

ALEXANDER enters, smiling and at ease. He is fifty-
two, boyish, handsome in the 1940's filmstar mould,
very obviously a gentleman, great social ease and
charm, loved by everyone from Prime Ministers to
charwomen.

130.   (CONTINUED)

                              ALEXANDER
                    Good morning, sir !

                              BROOKE
                    Hallo, Alex !

                              CHURCHILL
                    How delightful to see you !
                    Just off the plane ? Come and
                    have some breakfast.

Ushering him to little table where they have been
having theirs.

                    We're just off to the airport
                    ourselves ...

131.   THE SAME. H.Q. MIDDLE EAST. THE C-IN-C's ROOM

Conclusion of breakfast.

CHURCHILL is scribbling a memorandum on a piece of
Embassy letterhead.

                              CHURCHILL
                    There we are. That's what you've
                    got to do, Alex.

                              ALEXANDER
                              (reading it)
                    "Your prime and main duty will be
                    to take or destroy at the earliest
                    opportunity the German-Italian Army
                    commanded by Field Marshal Rommel
                    together with all its supplies and
                    establishments in North Africa."

                              CHURCHILL
                    And let me know when you've done it.

                              ALEXANDER
                    It might leak out anyhow, sir.

                              CHURCHILL
                              (rising)
                    Montgomery is arriving later today.
                    Give him all he wants.

131.   (CONTINUED)

> BROOKE
> He's never actually served under
> you, has he ?

> ALEXANDER
> No.

> BROOKE
> My advice is - give him his head.
> Rommel's planning to break through
> any day now.

CHURCHILL walking up and down.

> CHURCHILL
> Rommel, Rommel, Rommel ! What
> else matters but beating him !

132.   <u>EXT. DESERT H.Q. TENT SET UP FOR MONTGOMERY</u>

MONTGOMERY mounting a small box and addressing the
assembled SENIOR OFFICERS.

> MONTGOMERY
> My name's Montgomery, and I'm
> taking charge of this Army <u>now</u>.
> I'm not supposed to do so for
> three days, but I've sent the
> acting commander packing, and
> cabled Cairo to tell them what
> I've done. It's rank disobedience,
> and let me say here and now that
> anyone trying that sort of thing
> with me will finish up in very hot
> water indeed.
>
> Well now, you chaps seem to have
> got things into a bit of a mess.
> All that's going to change. All
> previous orders about withdrawal
> are cancelled; <u>this</u> is where we're
> going to fight, and if we can't
> stay alive here, then we'll stay
> here dead.
>
> That's going to take a lot of
> reorganisation and staff work.
> By the time the Prime Minister
> visits us again in a few days,

132. (CONTINUED)

> MONTGOMERY
> (cont'd)
> we'll have a new attitude in
> this Army, and a new strategy
> for the Western Desert. We're
> going to win this battle,
> transform the Middle East
> situation, smash the Africa
> Corps, knock Wommel for six,
> clear North Africa, and win the
> war, any questions ?

Utter silence

> Right.

He climbs down.

133.   INT.   OVAL ROOM.   WHITE HOUSE

EISENHOWER, MARSHALL, ISMAY and OTHER MEMBERS of the
Joint Chiefs of Staff Committee, round a conference
table which bears a large map of Northern Africa
and Egypt.

EISENHOWER is discussing Operation 'Torch', for the
invasion of Morocco and Tunisia.

He is fifty-two, tremendously alert and sure of
himself, frank, sincere and friendly.

> IKE
> Initially, the invasion of
> French North Africa must appear
> to be exclusively American, because
> we will be welcomed in Vichy
> territory, whereas I'm told the
> British will not. We have
> sufficient combat troops for
> only two landings - Casablanca
> and Oran. We must take Casablanca
> because we need a shore base on
> the North West coast, in case
> Gibraltar is blocked by the Nazis
> when we land.

IKE demonstrates all this on the map.

> ISMAY
> That's very interesting.

133. (CONTINUED)

>   MARSHALL
>   What's your reaction to it,
>   General Ismay ?
>
>   ISMAY
>   I rather think the British
>   Chiefs of Staff would wish for a
>   landing further East - Algiers, say.
>   (he points)
>   I'm not sure that you're right
>   about the nature of our reception
>   here.
>   (points)
>   But as we will be providing the
>   naval and air units, plus a not
>   inconsiderable invasion force,
>   why don't we land at all three
>   places, General Eisenhower ?
>
>   IKE
>   Why not ?
>
>   MARSHALL
>   I've no objection.
>
>   ISMAY
>   And the rapid tie-up with the
>   8th Army ?

He points to Libya.

>   MARSHALL
>   We can always hope.
>
>   ISMAY
>   Hmm.
>   (he grimaces)

They pour over the map.

>   One thing puzzles me. I thought
>   you'd decided to press ahead with
>   the landings in Northern France
>   first ?
>
>   MARSHALL
>   (awkward)
>   Well ... we need to show the
>   American people that we're not
>   just sitting on our rear ends
>   over here.

133. (CONTINUED)

> ISMAY
> Nothing to do with the
> forthcoming elections, then.

> MARSHALL /
> IKE
> (together)
> Oh no no, nothing like that !

134. INT. DESERT H.Q. TENT SET UP FOR MONTGOMERY - NIGHT

The tent is lit by hurricane lamps.

MONTGOMERY is engaged in a breathless exposition over a large scale battle map, almost racing from side to side of the table in his enthusiasm.

CHURCHILL is clearly delighted beyond words. It is like looking back on his own enthusiasm of May 1940.

BROOKE is also present.

> MONTGOMERY
> ... what Wommel likes best, you
> see, is to get our armour to attack
> him; he then puts his armour behind
> a screen of anti-tank guns, knocks
> out our tanks, and gets the field
> to himself. So I shall hold Alam
> Halfa ridge with the 44th and locate
> my tanks just south of the Western
> End. Wommel will penetrate my
> South front with a turn North towards
> the centre. I shall have four
> hundred tanks dug in and deployed
> behind six-pounder anti-tank guns.
> This line will not move ..... and
> they will be allowed to beat up
> against it and suffer heavy casualties
> before withdrawing. We've actually
> rehearsed this.

> CHURCHILL
> Rehearsed it ?

> MONTGOMERY
> With the thirty-first Group pretending
> to be Wommel's armour. I've got the
> exact route he'll take pegged out.
> With little pegs, like this one.

134.   (CONTINUED)

>   CHURCHILL
What if he doesn't take it ?

>   MONTGOMERY
He will, he will, or he's not
the man I thought.
>   (he splutters with
>   amusement)
Then we'll counter-attack, when
we're ready.

>   BROOKE
And you say Rommel will attack
on September the first.

>   MONTGOMERY
At one a.m., yes. All factors
point to that.

>   CHURCHILL
How long after the defensive
battle will you yourself attack ?

>   MONTGOMERY
Seven weeks.

>   CHURCHILL
What ?

>   BROOKE
>   (hastily)
You must accept seven weeks, sir.

>   MONTGOMERY
We shall punch two corridors
through their lines with our new
Spearhead Group, here and here.
>   (he demonstrates)
We'd develop around this area,
and destroy the Africa Corps from
behind.

CHURCHILL looks up like a delighted child at these
words.

He growls and purrs, pawing over the map.

>   BROOKE
May I suggest, sir, that the
greatest service we can do for
General Montgomery now, is to go
back to London as planned and
leave him alone ?

134. (CONTINUED)

CHURCHILL looks at BROOKE; grunts to himself, and nods.

On an impulse, he suddenly ruffles MONTGOMERY's hair, and chuckles.

135. NEWSFILM

Loading and preparation for the 'Torch' Invasion Force, at night.

                    ROOSEVELT (V.O.)
          Roosevelt to General Eisenhower.
          Please pass my best wishes on to
          the North African invasion fleet.
          The peace of the world depends on
          them. All America praying for you.

136. INT. CHURCHILL'S BEDROOM

CHURCHILL and BROOKE alone.

The tension of waiting for news. A good deal of brandy in evidence.

                    CHURCHILL
          Do you suppose the telephone is
          functioning all right ?

BROOKE lifts it, listens to the dialling tone, replaces it.

CHURCHILL walks about.

          How can Alexander remain in Cairo,
          with such great events impending
          in the desert ? - A battle that
          could reverse the course of the
          entire war ?

                    BROOKE
          You're so sure of victory, sir ?

                    CHURCHILL
          Well ....

He leaves it unsaid. He walks about.

136. (CONTINUED)

> BROOKE
> What have you felt deprived of
> most in this war, sir ?

> CHURCHILL
> Time to paint. And you ?

> BROOKE
> Time with my wife and children.
> I spent Sunday morning with them
> mending their goat-cart, while
> they chattered about. I hadn't
> seen them in eight months.

> CHURCHILL
> I miss the bells, too.

> BROOKE
> The church bells ?

> CHURCHILL
> (nods)
> Do you know, it's two years now,
> since I ordered them to be silent ?
> I think the bells of England the
> sweetest sound God ever made.
> Apart from our children's voices.
> I've told Alex we'll order all the
> bells to be rung again, if he and
> Eisenhower succeed.

> BROOKE
> Yes, he told me.

> CHURCHILL
> I miss bricklaying, too. I did
> a lot of bricklaying in my house
> in Kent. Bricking is so regular
> and orderly ... qualities for
> which, as you know, I am well known.

Silence.

He suddenly waves both fists in the air, and howls
aloud -

> How can we sit here, with Alex and
> Monty having all the fun ?

137.   INT. DESERT H.Q. TENT SET UP FOR MONTGOMERY - NIGHT

PANNING ACROSS the tent at night.   Silence.
MONTGOMERY asleep in his camp bed.

138.   NEWSFILM

Darkness of the desert. Then sudden flare and roar
of German guns as they start their offensive.

139.   INT. DESERT H.Q. TENT SET UP FOR MONTGOMERY

SENIOR OFFICER on duty comes in a hurry and shakes
MONTY awake.

                    OFFICER
          Sir ! Sir ! The German
          offensive has begun !

MONTY sits up, listens, checks his watch.

                    MONTY
          Excellent, couldn't be better.

He lies down and goes to sleep again.

140.   NEWSFILM

The Battle of Alam Halfa.

ROMMEL being pulverised and driven back by the static
tanks.

                    MONTGOMERY (V.O.)
          Montgomery to Pwime Minister.
          Wommel kept exactly to my little
          pegs. Now retreating with bloody
          nose. We shall now prepare our
          own advance.

141. <u>NEWFILM</u>

'Torch' Landings.

> IKE (V.O.)
> Eisenhower to Joint Chiefs of
> Staff. First wave of 'Torch'
> landing at Casablanca, Oran and
> Algiers. Encountering little
> resistance.

141a. H.Q. MIDDLE EASTERN COMMAND. CAIRO

ALEXANDER dictating:

> ALEXANDER
> Commander Middle East to Montgomery.
> I think you should know that
> Intelligence reports German troops
> are being switched from your front
> to reinforce Algeria and Tunisia.
> The following corps are involved ...

142. <u>NEWSFILM</u>

9.40 p.m. 23rd October 1942. The absolute silence of
the desert.

1000 heavy guns of the 8th Army open up simultaneously,
and the armour surges forward.

> MONTGOMERY (V.O.)
> Montgomery to Alexander. Battle
> of El Alamein launched spot on
> time.

143. <u>NEWSFILM</u>

The naval landings at Oran and Algiers - rough going
in the heavy surf.

> IKE (V.O.)
> Eisenhower to Chiefs of Staff.
> Naval invasion fleet successful
> landing. Resistance weakening.
> Operation Torch all going to plan.

144. NEWSFILM

The Battle of Alamein at its turning point.

Extremely heavy fighting.

> MONTGOMERY (V.O.)
> Montgomery to Pwime Minister.
> 8th Army broken right through
> Wommel's centre and developing.

145. NEWSFILM

Development of Torch - the parachute landings.

> IKE (V.O.)
> Operation Torch making rapid
> progress into Tunisia. Secondary
> wave air landing successful.
> Have firm hold.

146. NEWSFILM

El Alamein: the breakout.

> MONTGOMERY
> Wommel's forces broken, in full
> flight Westwards. Wommel on the
> run, Wommel on the run !

147. HEADQUARTERS, MIDDLE-EAST COMMAND, CAIRO

ALEXANDER reading this field-message.

He dictates:

> ALEXANDER
> Alexander to Prime Minister.
> (quiet understatement)
> Ring out the Bells.

148. INT. CHURCHILL'S BEDROOM

CHURCHILL being woken up in bed.

He grabs the proferred telegram and tears it open.

He reads it in silence, and does not move.

149. NEWSFILM

The BELLS of England ringing out.

ACT NINE

150. NEWSFILM

Night. A solitary plane seen flying high up in the
night sky, without escort.

151. INT. PLANE

Night. Inside the Liberator plane, with all its seats
removed.

PANNING OVER BROOKE, ISMAY, WILSON and OTHERS, curled
up in blankets on the floor or in chairs, trying to
sleep.

The steady drone of the plane.

TRACK INTO CLOSE SHOT CHURCHILL lying awake in the
half-light, eyes open, in his own nervous thoughts.

After a while, CHURCHILL starts taking his own pulse.

BROOKE, also lying awake, becomes aware that one of
the heaters is starting to smoke. He gets out of his
blankets and crawls on all fours to examine it.

                    CHURCHILL
          What is it ?

                    BROOKE
          This heater is red hot. The
          petrol fumes may burst into flames.

                    WILSON
          You've got to have heating - we're
          seven thousand feet up in mid-
          winter !

151. (CONTINUED)

> CHURCHILL
> It is dangerous.

BROOKE switches it off.

> I would sooner freeze to death than
> roast. Or drown, if we are still
> over the Atlantic.

BROOKE crawls back into his blankets.

> How long now ?

WILSON peers at his watch in the gloom.

> WILSON
> Three and a half hours.

> CHURCHILL
> (whisper)
> Do you think my strength will last
> out the war, Charles ? I sometimes
> feel I'm nearly spent. I kept the
> fight going until the Americans
> came in - perhaps I should retire
> now, withdraw from the scene and
> leave them to it, what do you
> think ?

WILSON snorts with amusement.

> But there's nothing left for me
> to do !

BROOKE has struggled up onto one elbow, in his blankets.

> BROOKE
> There'll be plenty for you to do
> at Casablanca, sir.

> CHURCHILL
> (gloomy)
> Just another conference. I've lost
> control.

> BROOKE
> I've been warned that the
> Americans may want to veto our
> entire Mediterranean strategy,
> and launch an invasion of Northern
> France this year, whether we like
> it or not.

151. (CONTINUED)

CHURCHILL sits up, astonished, galvanised into outrage.

> CHURCHILL
> What ? When, who told you that ?

> BROOKE
> Jack Dill said they'd been
> discussing it.

> CHURCHILL
> It would be catastrophic !
> A premature invasion of France -

> ISMAY
> (waking)
> I didn't trouble you with this,
> sir, because they have not
> decided whether it is to be
> their policy or not.

> BROOKE
> That's right.

> CHURCHILL
> (boiling)
> It could lose us the entire war !

> WILSON
> Winston, sit down and put some
> blankets over you ! You can do
> nothing about it up here.

They roll and crawl back into their blankets, and
lie there.

> CHURCHILL
> (sotto voce)
> Brookie ? Did Dill say who was
> behind it ?

> BROOKE
> He said General Marshall.

> CHURCHILL
> (after thought)
> We must prevent it. We must
> start by treating them purry-
> purry, puss-puss.

152.   INT.   THE ANFA HOTEL.   CASABLANCA

The hotel is a few miles outside Casablanca itself,
on the coast. The sea can be heard outside the open
windows.

Gathered around the table are: CHURCHILL, ROOSEVELT,
MARSHALL, EISENHOWER, HOPKINS, BROOKE, ISMAY,
ALEXANDER and OTHER SENIOR OFFICERS.

There is an atmosphere of antipathy and mistrust
between the two sides, veiled beneath a rather
strained politeness.

> MARSHALL
> ... leaving the central question
> to be decided between us as
> follows: when the British 8th
> Army and the Americans have
> fought their way across the
> desert to join up with each
> other, and between them have
> destroyed the enemy in North
> Africa; should we then strike
> across the Mediterranean and
> fight our way up into Central
> Europe from beneath; or should
> we close down the Mediterranean
> theatre altogether and throw
> everything we've got into a
> massive invasion of Northern
> Europe from the British Isles.

> CHURCHILL
> (beaming)
> Or both.

> ROOSEVELT
> (surprised)
> We don't have the facilities to
> do both, Winston, you know that.

> BROOKE
> The British position is that it
> is far too soon to attempt a
> Northern Europe invasion.

> MARSHALL
> I disagree.

152.   (CONTINUED)

                              BROOKE
                    We should follow up the success
                    of Alamein and Torch, by making
                    a rapid spring at Italy the
                    moment the Axis powers have been
                    eliminated from Africa.

                              CHURCHILL
                              (with relish)
                    It is the soft underbelly of
                    Hitler's Europe. Such an invasion
                    would break the crumbling morale
                    of Italy, throw the Balkans into
                    a ferment and may well bring Turkey
                    into the war. We should then
                    advance into Central and South
                    Eastern Europe by way of its soft
                    vitals.

The Americans have been listening with cool politeness.

                              ROOSEVELT
                              (very friendly)
                    That's a very interesting idea.
                    But we think anything other than
                    a massive invasion of France is
                    just nibbling at the edges.

                              CHURCHILL
                    "Nibbling" ?

                              ISMAY
                    Surely there's a great deal to be
                    said for continuing the impetus
                    of a victorious army ?

Silence.

                              IKE
                    May I ask a straight question,
                    sir ?

                              ROOSEVELT
                    Go ahead, General Eisenhower.

                              IKE
                    Do the British Chiefs of Staff
                    believe in an invasion of North
                    West Europe, or do they not ?

                              BROOKE
                              (snap)
                    Of course we do - at the right
                    time.

152.   (CONTINUED)

>   ROOSEVELT
>   And it has long been agreed in
>   principle between us ?

>   CHURCHILL
>   Oh certainly, certainly ... at
>   the right time.

He smiles at the Americans disarmingly. A rather
hostile silence.

MARSHALL decides to play his next card:

>   MARSHALL
>   My worry is this. If the drain
>   of men and armaments to the
>   Mediterranean means we could not
>   launch an invasion of France
>   this year, American public opinion
>   may demand that we switch our
>   major effort to the Pacific.

CHURCHILL is startled and offended.

MARSHALL and he look at each other across the table,
sizing each other up.

153.   EXT. BALCONY. CONFERENCE ROOM

A recess in the Conference.

British and Americans are gathered in small huddles
at either end of the room.

CHURCHILL sits in his braces, with bottle of wine.
BROOKE, ISMAY and ALEXANDER sit on the table or floor,
or stand about. They keep their voices down.

>   CHURCHILL
>   (exasperated)
>   But why attack Fortress Europe
>   at its most powerfully defended
>   point ?

>   BROOKE
>   We shall have to do so ultimately -

>   CHURCHILL
>   The slaughter would be appalling.

153. (CONTINUED)

> BROOKE
> - but only after thorough
> preparation, Marshall seems
> unable to comprehend that.

> ALEXANDER
> Or Eisenhower.

> BROOKE
> (snort)
> Eisenhower has no strategic
> sense at all.

> ALEXANDER
> (chuckle)
> Oh come, Brookie ...

> BROOKE
> To make a fruitless assault
> before the time is ripe, could
> extend the war by years !

> CHURCHILL
> And we've seen it all before.
> The whole of France a bloody
> slaughterhouse, the flower of
> English youth smashed to pieces
> at 60,000 a day ! I saw it, we
> all saw it; God forbid we should
> ever allow it again.

Pause. He suddenly pounds his knees.

> Northern France is the one place
> we could still <u>lose</u> this war !

154. <u>INT. CASABLANCA. CONFERENCE ROOM</u>

ROOSEVELT and MARSHALL talking quietly together at
the other end.

> MARSHALL
> Northern France is the one place
> we could still win this war
> quickly ! Six months to mount
> the operation -

154.   (CONTINUED)

                              ROOSEVELT
                    No, George - the drain of supplies
                    to North Africa makes it out of the
                    question this year. We'll go for
                    1944; May 1944.

                              MARSHALL
                    With no further extension of the
                    Mediterranean campaign meanwhile ?

                              ROOSEVELT
                              (wry)
                    We may have to compromise over
                    that one.

155.   EXT. SEASHORE

ALEXANDER with BROOKE, walking along the water's edge,
spotting birds. WILSON trails along behind them.

A HUGE SEABIRD takes off from the sands.

                              BROOKE
                    He told me once how he has a
                    recurring nightmare about the
                    massacre at Gallipoli.

                              WILSON
                    He told me about that. The shallow
                    water was thick with bodies, and
                    the sea absolutely red with blood
                    for a full 50 yards from the shore
                    right along the assault beaches.

                              ALEXANDER
                    And that was the result of hastily
                    prepared troops assaulting power-
                    fully held shore defences, from
                    the sea.

                              BROOKE
                    Exactly.

They walk on.

                              ALEXANDER
                    And he was held to be responsible ?

                              WILSON
                              (nods)
                    By a great many people.

                              BROOKE
                    Dear God.

156. <u>INT. CONFERENCE ROOM</u>

MARSHALL and EISENHOWER working through backlog of
military reports and cables at the conference table.

                    MARSHALL
               Do you think he's lost his nerve ?

                    IKE
               Churchill ?

                    MARSHALL
                  (nods)
               He now seems scared of exactly
               the sort of boldness he was
               advocating to the British in 1940.

EISENHOWER thinks for a while.

                    IKE
               I think it's more that he dislikes
               being tied down to a massive plan
               so far ahead. He prefers a sort
               of hand-to-mouth military
               opportunism. He's a swashbuckler,
               an adventurer.

                    MARSHALL
               Hmm. Maybe. But I wonder
               sometimes, if he's just not up to
               it any more.

A knock at the door, and CHURCHILL puts his head in.
He is at his most charming and mischievous.

                    CHURCHILL
               May I come in ?

                    MARSHALL
                  (rising)
               Mr. Churchill !

                    CHURCHILL
                  (entering)
               I hope I don't enter at an
               inconvenient moment ...

                    IKE
               If you will excuse me, sir ...

156.   (CONTINUED)

                              CHURCHILL
               No, no, I should like you to stay,
               if General Marshall has no
               objection. We may need a little
               assistance with this.

He holds up a bottle and glasses.

                              MARSHALL
               I hope you have not come to
               discuss where our next theatre
               of operations may be ?

                              CHURCHILL
               I suppose it might conceivably
               wander into the conversation,
               hahaha.

                              MARSHALL
               It's the President you should be
               discussing that with.

                              CHURCHILL
               He surely goes by what you say.

                              MARSHALL
               I give him military advice, when
               he asks for it.

                              CHURCHILL
               And very excellent advice it is
               too.
                         (he hands out glasses
                          of champagne)
               I came to tell you that I think
               I was quite wrong to imply any
               lack of enthusiasm for Operation
               Overlord. I wish to offer
               immediate cooperation for the
               landings in Northern France.

MARSHALL highly suspicious.

                              MARSHALL
               In what year ?

                              CHURCHILL
                         (beaming)
               As soon as practicable.

                              IKE
               That's rather an elastic term,
               sir.

156. (CONTINUED)

                              CHURCHILL
                    Well, we have been planning it
                    ourselves since 1941 - let us
                    compare our plans and agree to
                    a timetable, what do you say ?

                              IKE
                              (watching him)
                    And in return ?

                              CHURCHILL
                              (chuckle)
                    My dear sir .... !

                              IKE
                    But perhaps you have something
                    in mind ?

                              CHURCHILL
                    Well, in the same spirit of
                    cooperation, I would be delighted
                    to receive your approval of the
                    invasion of Sicily, as soon as
                    the Axis have been expelled from
                    North Africa.

EISENHOWER and MARSHALL rapidly trying to work it
all out.

CHURCHILL is still bouncing round the room:

                    Oh - another thing. We have not
                    yet decided the question of who
                    should be the Supreme Commander
                    of the combined force.

                              IKE
                    Surely that is self-evident,
                    sir.

                              CHURCHILL
                    Indeed ?

                              IKE
                    The British have twice as many
                    troops involved as we do; and
                    Alexander is a far more
                    experienced general than -

156.   (CONTINUED)

                         CHURCHILL
            Nevertheless, I shall propose to
            the President that you, General
            Eisenhower, should take over the
            Supreme Command, Mediterranean,
            with Alexander as your deputy.
                    (he beams)
            How are your glasses ?

EISENHOWER and MARSHALL even more suspicious.

157.   INT. CONFERENCE ROOM - NIGHT

Low lighting.

ROOSEVELT and HOPKINS sit close together. The others
are gathering for the next session of the conference.

                         HOPKINS
            What is he up to ?

                         ROOSEVELT
            You don't trust him, Harry ?

                         HOPKINS
            When he resorts to guile, no-one
            can do better than Winston
            Churchill.

                         ROOSEVELT
            What did Marshall think ?

                         HOPKINS
            That it was simply a ploy to
            stop us switching everything
            to the Pacific.

A sudden beep-beep noise outside, a hooter.

            Air-raid warning. They'll put
            out the lights in a minute.

A SERVANT comes in and starts to light candles in
bottles on conference table, and put out overhead
lights.

                         ROOSEVELT
            Maybe we should give a little
            this time.

158.   INT.   CONFERENCE ROOM - NIGHT

Six candles in bottles on the table, giving an eerie
light to the final session of the Conference.

The DRONE of enemy planes can be heard overhead.

                    ROOSEVELT
          ... our inability to agree
          wholeheartedly on the next stage
          of the war. As chairman, I
          therefore propose that we should
          continue to clear North Africa,
          and proceed to take Sicily; but
          we should meet again at the
          conclusion of the African campaign
          to decide our next move, in the
          light of the situation as it then
          appears.

                    MARSHALL
          Leaving open the question of -
          Where next ?

                    ROOSEVELT
          Exactly.

                    BROOKE
          Meanwhile a timetable is to be
          agreed for Operation Overlord.

                    ROOSEVELT
          Yes.

                    HOPKINS
                    (pointedly)
          May I ask Mr. Churchill if he
          accepts this ?

CHURCHILL turns on him with some annoyance.

                    CHURCHILL
          Let me make one thing quite clear.
          I have heard a rumour here that
          the British wish to scuttle
          'Overlord'. That is not so. I
          have given my word, and will keep
          it. But we shall shortly have
          glorious opportunities in the
          Mediterranean theatre - and it
          would be madness not to seize
          them ! When the time comes for
          the landings in Northern France,
          you will not find us wanting.

158. (CONTINUED)

>   MARSHALL
>   "When the time comes" ?

CHURCHILL's temper suddenly snaps

>   CHURCHILL
>   Those were my words, sir !

A rather chilly silence.

>   ROOSEVELT
>   I have drawn up a brief summary
>   of the main points of our
>   agreement to send to Marshall
>   Stalin, Winston. If you would
>   care to sign them ...

CHURCHILL examines the document with great care and
suspicion, as if he was afraid of being cheated.

There is an icy silence on both sides.

Drone of enemy planes overhead, and some distant
Ack-Ack fire.

A C T   T E N

159. NEWSFILM

The joining up of the American Army and the British
8th Army across the desert, April 1943.

Joint celebrations: sharing each other's tanks and
armoured cars, swopping chewing gum for British
cigarettes, swopping hats, etc.

Slogans chalked on the side of tanks and guns -
"Welcome to the world's second biggest Army"
"Welcome to the world's second best"
"Look out Rommel, here we come" etc.

160. INT. OFFICE IN EISENHOWER'S VILLA, ALGERIA

Crossed American and British flags hang on the wall
behind his desk.

ALEXANDER and MONTGOMERY are entering in full uniform,
and salute him.

                    ALEXANDER
          With the joining-up of the
          British and American forces,
          sir, we should like to congratulate
          you on your appointment as Supreme
          Commander, North Africa, and to
          express our consciousness of the
          high honour of serving under your
          command.

                    MONTGOMERY
          Absolutely.

                    IKE
          Gentlemen, I appreciate that very
          much. And I must tell you how
          humble I feel at having two such
          very fine Generals under my
          command.

160. (CONTINUED)

                                MONTGOMERY
                    I shouldn't let that worry you,
                    sir. Actually, I've drawn
                    up some notes here ...
                              (he extracts typed
                              document from
                              briefcase)
                    ... how to finish the North
                    African campaign pretty quickly,
                    by mopping up Tunisia. It's
                    quite straightforward.
                              (hands document
                              over)
                    You'll find my requirements
                    listed on page fourteen.

                                IKE
                    That's very courteous of you,
                    General. Please sit down.

ALEXANDER and MONTGOMERY are delighted EISENHOWER
is taking this attitude.

                    I'm sorry to raise a distasteful
                    matter at our first meeting, but
                    it's the cornerstone of my
                    beliefs that British and
                    American should work so closely
                    together that there is no
                    distinction between them. So
                    I regret that some Americans
                    regard themselves as crusaders,
                    come to help Europe out of a
                    mess ...
                              (he is growing angry
                              as he speaks)
                    I won't have that. Not in my
                    command. That is why I dismissed
                    my liaison officer to the 8th
                    Army from his position and from
                    my staff.

                                ALEXANDER
                    Wasn't it a bit drastic ?

                                IKE
                    Not at all. He was going round
                    drunk saying we would show the
                    British how to fight. He also
                    insulted a brother-officer.

160. (CONTINUED)

>   MONTGOMERY
>   He only called him a son-of-a-
>   bitch, didn't he ?

>   IKE
>   (hissing)
>   He called him a British son-of-
>   a-bitch. That's unforgivable !
>   If we two nations fight each
>   other, Hitler could still pull
>   it off.

161. INT. CHURCHILL'S BEDROOM

CHURCHILL, working at papers, in bed, cigar in mouth.
He coughs and holds his chest, feeling none too well.

A KNOCK, and BROOKE enters, immaculate as always, and
crosses to stand by him.

>   BROOKE
>   You wished to see me, sir.

>   CHURCHILL
>   (not looking up)
>   Sit down.

BROOKE does, and waits.

CHURCHILL finally turns to him.

>   How do you view an Italian
>   invasion in relation to the
>   invasion of Northern France -
>   Operation 'Overlord' ?

>   BROOKE
>   (very concise)
>   'Overlord' is the key to
>   victory, but an Italian
>   campaign is an indispensable
>   preliminary.

>   CHURCHILL
>   Humph. I should like you to
>   take over the Supreme Command
>   of 'Overlord', at a suitable
>   moment.

BROOKE is hardened to sudden elevation, but even so,
his head swims.

>   Well ? What do you say ?

161.   (CONTINUED)

                              BROOKE
              I ... I don't know what to say !

                              CHURCHILL
                              (growl)
              You turned down my offers of
              command before.

                              BROOKE
              I turned down the 8th Army and
              the Middle East command, because
              we were at a low point, and my
              place was at your side.

                              CHURCHILL
              To keep me "Under Control".

                              BROOKE
              Yes, sir.

                              CHURCHILL
              And now ?

                              BROOKE
                              (pause)
              Now the end is in sight.

CHURCHILL positively glows at these words, purring
like a cat.

              Has Roosevelt agreed ?

                              CHURCHILL
              He agreed to an American
              Supreme Commander for North
              Africa. I made sure of that.

                              BROOKE
              And ... now it's "Our Turn" ?

                              CHURCHILL
                              (ignoring this)
              You realise it's the great
              Command of the War ? - the
              biggest invasion-by-sea in the
              entire history of warfare ?

                              BROOKE
              Yes.

161. (CONTINUED)

                              CHURCHILL
                  Yes. Child's play, after all
                  the years of putting up with me,
                  eh ?

He gives a throaty chuckle, and pats BROOKE's knee
with affection.

                  Run along now. Keep it secret.

He turns back to his work, coughing with the first
signs of Pneumonia.

162. NEWSFILM

The end of the North African campaign - 250,000 Axis
soldiers laying down their arms and trudging miserably
to the huge prisoner 'cages' in the desert.

British and American troops celebrate.

The desert is littered with shot-up German tanks,
armoured cars, burned-out planes, guns, as far as the
eye can see. Bodies lie everywhere.

                              ALEXANDER (V.O.)
                  General Alexander to Prime
                  Minister. Sir, the orders you
                  gave me on August 15th, 1942
                  have been fulfilled. His
                  Majesty's enemies together with
                  their impedimentia have been
                  completely eliminated from
                  Egypt, Cyrenaica, Libya and
                  Tripolitania. We are now
                  masters of the North African
                  shores.   I await your further
                  instructions.

163. INT. CHURCHILL'S BEDROOM

CHURCHILL flinging his bedclothes off and lurching out
of bed to get dressed, scattering reports and papers in
every direction.

                              WILSON
                          (angry)
                  You can't go to America !

163. (CONTINUED)

> CHURCHILL
> (shout)
> I have to go to America !
>
> WILSON
> You've got pneumonia ! You
> know what they call it - Old
> Man's Friend.
>
> CHURCHILL
> What ? Why ?
>
> WILSON
> Because it carries them off so
> quickly.
>
> CHURCHILL
> Well, I'm going !

164. <u>NEWSFILM</u>

The Queen Mary (converted to a troop-carrier) sounding
her ship's horn, as she steams out into the Atlantic.

165. <u>INT. OVAL ROOM. WHITE HOUSE</u>

A conference table, round which are seated CHURCHILL,
BROOKE, ISMAY, MARSHALL, ROOSEVELT, HOPKINS, STIMSON
and ADVISERS.

It is stiflingly hot. Everyone is in shirtsleeves,
and the windows are wide open.

It is clear that the mistrust of the Casablanca
Conference has hardened to positive antagonism.

CHURCHILL and MARSHALL face each other from opposite
ends of the conference table. CHURCHILL, though better,
is still far from well.

BROOKE is putting his usual rapid, staccato quickfire
military arguments.

165.   (CONTINUED)

                    BROOKE
        ... until the U-Boat menace is
        overcome, shortage of shipping
        alone must remain a stranglehold
        on all offensive operations
        against the French coast. With
        the twenty-one divisions that
        General Marshall contemplates,
        any invasion would be easily
        repelled by the far more
        numerous German divisions
        already in North West Europe.

MARSHALL is seen to restrain his irritation with
difficulty.

        Frontal attack on that sort of
        defence is suicide.

                  STIMSON
            (mock-incredulous)
        Yet you say you are ultimately
        for such an invasion !

                    BROOKE
        After adequate preparations,
        Mr. Stimson.

                  STIMSON
        Then for God's sake let's
        concentrate everything on
        making them _now_ !

                 CHURCHILL
        But it would be criminal not
        to seize the great prizes
        awaiting us in the _Mediterranean_ -

The Americans almost howl with exasperation.

        - the Italian Fleet and the
        twenty-six Divisions with which
        Italy is garrisoning the Balkans
        would both be lost to Germany,
        the British Mediterranean Fleet
        would be released for action
        elsewhere -

                 MARSHALL
            (quickly)
        Where ?

                 CHURCHILL
            (evasive)
         Wherever required.

165.   (CONTINUED)

>   MARSHALL
>   The assault on France ?

CHURCHILL bulldozes his way through the question,
greatly irritated.

The Conference is fast becoming a head-on clash between
him and MARSHALL.

>   CHURCHILL
>   The greatest prize now is to
>   knock Italy out of the war by
>   whatever means !

>   MARSHALL
>   But the Nazis don't care a damn
>   about Italy ! In our opinion,
>   it's far more important to draw
>   off some of the enemy pressure
>   on the Russian front, by
>   establishing a second front
>   immediately !

>   CHURCHILL
>   Precisely what an Italian invasion
>   would do !

>   MARSHALL
>   No, sir !

>   CHURCHILL
>   There are 185 German divisions on
>   the Russian front - if we knocked
>   Italy out of the war, the Germans
>   would be forced to send back
>   large numbers of troops to hold
>   down the Balkans !

MARSHALL is immediately suspicious.

>   MARSHALL
>   Why the Balkans, Mr. Churchill ?

>   CHURCHILL
>   Heh ?

>   MARSHALL
>   You have no offensive plans for
>   the Balkans ?

>   CHURCHILL
>   (very angry)
>   We have disclosed our plans to
>   you !

165.   (CONTINUED)

> MARSHALL
> The "Backdoor into Germany" ?

CHURCHILL goes red with anger, and starts banging the table, furious.

> CHURCHILL
> My commanders have complained
> to me of the shortage of landing
> craft and carriers in the
> Mediterranean theatre; they
> wonder if these resources are
> being <u>deliberately</u> held back for
> any reason, General Marshall ?

166.   <u>INT.   OVAL ROOM</u>

ROOSEVELT, MARSHALL and HOPKINS, over a quick buffet lunch round the President's table.

> MARSHALL
> It's incredible ! - but he's
> still trying to prove he was
> right about Gallipoli.

> HOPKINS
> I don't follow.

> MARSHALL
> In the First World War.

> HOPKINS
> Of course, but I don't see ...

> MARSHALL
> He persuaded the British
> Cabinet to try to finish Germany
> quickly by a quick thrust up
> from the Mediterranean - via
> the Dardanelles, via Gallipoli.
> It was called "the Backdoor into
> Germany".

> ROOSEVELT
> No, George.

> MARSHALL
> It was a disaster, and he was
> dismissed. He's always maintained
> that the failure was due to bad
> execution, not because it was
> wrong in principle. <u>That's</u> what
> this is all about.

166. (CONTINUED)

> ROOSEVELT
> No, George, that's too
> fantastic.

> HOPKINS
> (walking round,
> growling)
> I don't think it matters a
> damn what his reasons are -
> his obstinacy is now <u>extending</u>
> this war !

167. INT. <u>SMALL PLAIN OFFICE, WHITE HOUSE</u>

CHURCHILL and BROOKE alone.

BROOKE working through his notes for the next session:
CHURCHILL deep in thought.

> CHURCHILL
> I want you to draw up a map
> tonight, showing further
> invasion points along the whole
> Northern side of the <u>Mediterranean</u>,
> Gibraltar to the Black Sea. Let
> me have it first thing tomorrow.

> BROOKE
> But I shall be up till 2 a.m.,
> preparing my speech !

CHURCHILL looks up at him, surprised.

> CHURCHILL
> Do it afterwards, then.

168. INT. <u>OVAL ROOM</u>

Evening of the following day. The Conference in
session.

It is cooler, but everyone is exhausted and inclined
to silliness.

168. (CONTINUED)

>   BROOKE
> ... and since the great bulk of
> troops in North Africa are
> British, I think we may exercise
> some claim as to how they should
> be used. You would not wish to
> attempt an invasion of France,
> on your own ?

>   MARSHALL
> No.

>   ISMAY
> But you are saying that every-
> thing should now be subordinated
> to a Second Front ?

>   MARSHALL
> Yes.

>   BROOKE
>   (giving up)
> Well, we don't agree.

Both sides sit back, having reached deadlock.

>   ROOSEVELT
> Perhaps we could examine the
> British plan for an invasion of
> Italy once more, in return for a
> commitment to a definite date to
> invade France.

He looks around for response to this.

>   ISMAY
> Obviously, we would need to
> consult before replying to that.

>   ROOSEVELT
> In that case, I suggest we
> adjourn at this point.

Generally exhausted, they rise and chatter.

ROOSEVELT turns to CHURCHILL

>   Whew !

>   CHURCHILL
>   (wipes brow)
> Boiling.

168.   (CONTINUED)

                              ROOSEVELT
                    We ought to draw up a list of
                    what we do agree about, for
                    Uncle Joe Stalin. Let's do
                    that tonight, over a glass of
                    wine.

CHURCHILL rolls his eyes at ROOSEVELT.

                              CHURCHILL
                    A glass ?

169.   INT. OVAL ROOM

The cool of the evening. A great many bottles on the
President's table.

ROOSEVELT and CHURCHILL, in shirtsleeves, sit at either
end of the otherwise empty conference table,
struggling to draft the 'points of agreement'.

The table and floor is littered with notes and
abandoned drafts.

Silence for a while - just groans of toil.

                              ROOSEVELT
                         (looking up)
                    Perhaps we ought to compromise.
                    Ike to draw up detailed plans to
                    invade Italy, in return for
                    pinning you down to May 1st 1944
                    to invade France, how about that ?

                              CHURCHILL
                    But when would we invade Italy ?

                              ROOSEVELT
                    Oh, after we'd taken Sicily, we'd
                    have another conference to decide
                    that.

CHURCHILL groans aloud.

                              CHURCHILL
                    These interminable conferences !
                    I'm a fighter, not a politician !

169.   (CONTINUED)

>   ROOSEVELT
>   (chuckle)
> You should talk to General
> Marshall about that ! He's a
> political philosopher as much
> as a soldier !

>   CHURCHILL
>   (interested)
> Really ?

>   ROOSEVELT
>   (nods)
> If you want to convince George
> about anything, it's the
> statesman in him you should
> appeal to !

CHURCHILL absorbs this information, immediately deciding
how he will tackle Marshall.

> In fact, he's the man to get in
> on these Points of Agreement -
> he's brilliant at that sort of
> thing.

>   CHURCHILL
> But when ? I'm off to Algeria
> at first light.

ROOSEVELT throws pencil down, and sits back, smiling.

>   ROOSEVELT
> Take him with you !

170.   INT.   FLYING BOAT

A great deal more roomy and comfortable than the old
seatless Liberator.

CHURCHILL is in a small cabin of his own, pouring over
a map of the Mediterranean on which Brooke has marked
alternative invasion routes from Tunisia - the Italian
coast East and West, the Adriatic, Yugoslavia, Greece,
Albania, Turkey, the Balkans, the Dardanelles, even
Romania via the Black Sea.

170. (CONTINUED)

    Other papers litter the table. There are the
inevitable cigars and bottle of white wine.

    A KNOCK at the door, and MARSHALL comes in. He
holds up a page of typescript.

                    MARSHALL
        I've summarised those points
        for Marshal Stalin, sir.

                    CHURCHILL
          (startled)
        What ?
          (he takes and reads
          it)
        Your President couldn't do this,
        even with my assistance.

                    MARSHALL
        Is it alright ?

Pause.

                    CHURCHILL
          (finishing)
        I congratulate you. We are
        most obliged.

                    MARSHALL
        Though I don't imagine you asked
        me to accompany you just for
        that, Mr. Churchill.

                    CHURCHILL
        No indeed.
          (he beams)
        I do wish you would call me
        Winston - I call you George,
        behind your back.

                    MARSHALL
        I never use first names.

                    CHURCHILL
        What, never ?

                    MARSHALL
        No, sir.

                    CHURCHILL
        Not even to your wife ?

170.   (CONTINUED)

                              MARSHALL
                            (deadpan)
                I may get around to first names
                with her, eventually.

CHURCHILL chuckles, and pours wine for them both.

MARSHALL is very much on his guard, knowing that
Churchill is about to try some new ploy to win him
round, and determined to resist.

This reserve accentuates his great natural dignity,
almost grandeur - 'the noblest Roman of them all'.
It is impossible to imagine him doing anything
mean or underhand.

                              CHURCHILL
                I asked you to come because I
                think it is a thousand pities
                that this antagonism should have
                arisen between us; and to discuss
                a certain matter which can only
                be spoken of in private.

                              MARSHALL
                You also wished me to see the
                enthusiasm of my own Generals
                in Algeria, to continue the
                fight in the Mediterranean.

                              CHURCHILL
                            (grin)
                I will not deny it.

                              MARSHALL
                Then it's the President you
                should have brought along.

                              CHURCHILL
                He fails to see any point in an
                invasion of Italy.

                              MARSHALL
                            (nods)
                He wants the twenty divisions
                which could be released after
                the conquest of Sicily, to be
                used to build up the Cross-
                Channel invasion force.

170.   (CONTINUED)

                              CHURCHILL
                          (growl)
                    And stand still, doing nothing,
                    for over a year ?

                              MARSHALL
                    The same old arguments, Mr.
                    Churchill ?

                              CHURCHILL
                    Yes, yes, you are right.

CHURCHILL sweeps cigar ash from the map, and turns
it round.

He speaks with his old attack and vigour:

                    If we invade here -
                          (points to the Balkans)
                    - and drive through to Germany, all
                    these states of Eastern Europe will
                    remain free, under our protection:
                    Bulgaria, Romania, Poland, Yugoslavia,
                    Czechoslovakia. But if we invade
                    here -
                          (points to Northern
                          France)
                    - then Russia will liberate those
                    countries as she advances from the
                    East, like this. A curtain of iron
                    will descend upon them, and they
                    will be enmeshed in the evil web
                    of communist totalitarianism, just
                    as much as if they were still under
                    the heel of the Nazis.

Silence.

MARSHALL looks at the map, digesting this. CHURCHILL
watches him closely for his reaction.

                              CHURCHILL
                    Naturally, you will have considered
                    this, and will have rejected such
                    considerations as not your business
                    as a soldier. But you are also an
                    American ... and you are deciding
                    the future of Europe.

Silence.

CHURCHILL watches him carefully.

170. (CONTINUED)

                    MARSHALL
          I should like to ask you a
          very straight question.

                    CHURCHILL
          Pray do so.

                    MARSHALL
          You seem to arrive at military
          decisions of the highest
          importance more by <u>instinct</u>
          than analysis.

                    CHURCHILL
          I think that is true.

                    MARSHALL
          What is your most basic reason
          for opposing the invasion of
          Northern France ?

CHURCHILL sits still and huddled for a minute;
MARSHALL is astonished to see tears in his eyes.

                    CHURCHILL
          I see the English Channel full
          of corpses.

Silence.

Then MARSHALL rises.

                    MARSHALL
          I will think over what you have
          said, sir.

                    CHURCHILL
          Pray do so.

                    MARSHALL
          It has nothing to do with
          military strategy.

                    CHURCHILL
          But everything to do with
          human life.

MARSHALL nods, stands there for a moment, and then
goes out.

171. INT. OFFICE IN EISENHOWER'S VILLA, ALGERIA

EISENHOWER behind his desk, standing, in full uniform.

An ORDERLY opens the door.

> ORDERLY
> General Montgomery, sir.

MONTGOMERY enters quickly, annoyed.

> MONTGOMERY
> I am not accustomed to being
> summoned in quite such a
> peremptory manner.

> IKE
> Even so, I believe it is the
> custom to salute, or say good
> morning ?

MONTGOMERY comes up with a jerk.

> MONTGOMERY
> I beg your pardon.
> (he salutes)
> Good morning, sir.

> IKE
> Good morning.
> (cool)
> You may sit down.

> MONTGOMERY
> (sitting)
> It happens to be a most
> inconvenient moment to leave
> my Tac H.Q. -

> IKE
> What's all this about a plane ?

> MONTGOMERY
> What ?

> IKE
> A Flying Fortress aircraft, for
> your personal use.

> MONTGOMERY
> Oh, that. General Bedell Smith
> said that if I cleared the
> Germans out of the town of
> Sousse by May 20th, I could have
> one, fully crewed, for my own use.

171.   (CONTINUED)

                              IKE
          It was a joke.

                              MONTGOMERY
          Oh, no.

                              IKE
          A jocular remark.

                              MONTGOMERY
          I did clear the town by that
          date, and I claim my aircraft.
          It will be immensely useful as
          a mobile H.Q.

                              IKE
          Bedell Smith also tells me that
          you have insisted on delivery
          by the 30th of this month.

                              MONTGOMERY
          Absolutely. It never crossed my
          mind that the Americans would fail
          to keep their word.

                              IKE
          I beg your pardon ?

                              MONTGOMERY
          We're not used to that sort of
          thing in the British Army.

          EISENHOWER keeps his temper with the greatest of
          difficulty.

                              IKE
          For the sake of Anglo-American
          relations, your aircraft will
          be delivered.

                              MONTGOMERY
          Oh good.

                              IKE
          You will, however, accept no
          further bets of this sort.

                              MONTGOMERY
          Now I have something here for
          you, sir ...
                    (rummages in briefcase)

                              IKE
          Have you any idea how much those
          things cost ?

171.　(CONTINUED)

>   MONTGOMERY
>   The Sicilian invasion plan,
>   Operation 'Husky'.
>   (he produces file)
>   It's a dog's breakfast. It
>   breaks every commonsense rule
>   of practical fighting, and
>   stands no chance at all of
>   success.

>   IKE
>   (frosty)
>   Put your comments on paper, and
>   I will read them.

>   MONTGOMERY
>   I've already done so.
>   (hands over a typed
>   report of ten pages)
>   I've also drawn up a much
>   better plan, that will knock
>   Sicily for six before you can
>   say Jack Wobinson.
>   (hands over typed
>   document)

>   IKE
>   Is that all, General ?

>   MONTGOMERY
>   Just one other thing. The man
>   who drew up that plan - is he
>   British or American ?

>   IKE
>   (full of hate)
>   I can't remember, but I'm sure
>   he'll appreciate your comments.

172.　NEWSFILM

The invasion of Sicily and the overthrow of Mussolini
which followed.

>   MARSHALL (V.O.)
>   Marshall to the President. I
>   have come to the conclusion that
>   there is substance in Mr.
>   Churchill's case for an invasion
>   of Southern Italy ...

We hear CHURCHILL's long, tired, and contented CHUCKLE.

173. INT. WHITE HOUSE. SMALL PLAIN ROOM

STIMSON addressing a meeting of the American Chiefs
of Staff.

He is forceful, angry, and determined to nail British
prevarication once and for all.

> STIMSON
> There are now no grounds left
> for the British to procrastinate
> further. Everything that matters
> has been gained in the Mediterranean.
> We should cease all operations
> there, now, this week, and throw
> everything we've got at France !

174. INT.WAR ROOM

CHURCHILL addressing a meeting of the British Chiefs
of Staff, with something of his old attack and relish.

> CHURCHILL
> The surrender of the Italian army
> at any moment, opens up the most
> momentous prospects in the Eastern
> Mediterranean ! Massive cracks
> are appearing in the German
> defences of South East Europe,
> offering gleaming prizes, which
> must be exploited to the full !

175. INT. WHITE HOUSE. SMALL PLAIN OFFICE

Meeting continues.

> STIMSON
> We can no longer accept a British
> commander for the Cross-Channel
> invasion. We should demand an
> American Commander, and we should
> impose on the British a timetable
> which they can no way wriggle
> out of !

176. INT. WAR ROOM

Meeting continues.

> CHURCHILL
> The most immediate prizes
> are the Greek islands. I am
> certain that once we have
> captured them, the Americans
> will give us their hearty
> support.

177. INT. WHITE HOUSE. OVAL ROOM

STIMSON with ROOSEVELT.

> STIMSON
> The Chiefs of Staff were
> unanimous that we must cut out
> all further Mediterranean
> diversions of whatever kind.
> And we must insist on American
> Supreme Command of Operation
> 'Overlord'.

He hands over a three-page typescript.

ROOSEVELT flicks through it.

> ROOSEVELT
> I entirely agree.

STIMSON delighted.

> STIMSON
> And no invasion of Italy ?

> ROOSEVELT
> We may have to make a token
> invasion, to bring about the
> final Italian surrender, but
> no more. I'll tell Churchill.

> STIMSON
> Tell him ?

> ROOSEVELT
> Tell him.

178. INT. BEDROOM

ISMAY has brought in Roosevelt's long telegram, and
stands waiting while CHURCHILL reads through it.

Just a desk lamp on in the dark room.

                    CHURCHILL
            What time is it ?

                    ISMAY
            11.30.

CHURCHILL turns a page, reads on.

                    CHURCHILL
            Has Brookie seen this ?

                    ISMAY
            Not yet.

179. INT. ANTE ROOM

BROOKE has pushed back the chair from his desk, very
tired, chatting to WILSON.

                    BROOKE
            You know he's talking about a quick
            dash to Moscow ? - and then off to
            Italy as soon as we land, wading
            about in the mud and slush ?

                    WILSON
            Out of the question !

                    BROOKE
            You tell him.

                    WILSON
            He's lost confidence in me.

                    BROOKE
                (chuckle)
            Nonsense.

                    WILSON
            He calls me the most awful things.

                    BROOKE
            Genius under intolerable pressure
            is impossible to live with -
            especially English genius.

179. (CONTINUED)

                              WILSON
                         (looking up)
                    Is that how you see it ?

                              BROOKE
                    Oh yes. He's quite the most
                    awful and quite the most wonderful
                    man I've ever met. Every month
                    with him is a year off my life,
                    yet I wouldn't miss a minute of it -
                    no-one would, no-one. You know,
                    I got two whole days holiday away
                    from him last year ? <u>Two</u> ?

                              WILSON
                    What did you do ?

                              BROOKE
                    Went grouse-shooting in Yorkshire.
                    When I got to my butt out on the
                    lonely rain-swept moor, I found
                    he'd installed a field telephone
                    in it with a direct line from
                    Downing Street.

ISMAY enters.

                              ISMAY
                    Excuse me, Brookie. The Prime
                    Minister wonders if you'd be
                    good enough to spare him a moment.

                              BROOKE
                         (rising)
                    Of course.

                              WILSON
                         (snort)
                    I bet he didn't put it like that !

                              ISMAY
                    Have you read Telegram 417 ?
                    From Roosevelt ?

BROOKE flicks through the relevant file on his desk.

                              BROOKE
                    Er - no, my copy's just come.

                              ISMAY
                         (gently)
                    It might be helpful if you read it
                    first.

BROOKE registers that something is amiss, finds telegram,
starts to read.

180. INT. WAR ROOM

Churchill's desk lamp on. Papers all over the table.
Rest of the room in semi-darkness.

CHURCHILL stands at the far end, in shadow, deep in
thought.

BROOKE enters.

>   CHURCHILL
>   Have you read it ?

>   BROOKE
>   Yes.

>   CHURCHILL
>   What do you think ?

>   BROOKE
>   Quite a shock.

CHURCHILL suddenly swings on him with excitement.

>   CHURCHILL
>   But don't you see, we'll agree
>   to the Americans running Overlord,
>   in return for letting us run the
>   Mediterranean - that way we can
>   launch our Greek Island venture
>   from a position of strength !

BROOKE fights down his personal feelings at losing the
Supreme Command in this offhand way, with great
difficulty.

>   BROOKE
>   World commands can't be exchanged
>   that quickly, sir. Besides, the
>   Americans would never agree.

>   CHURCHILL
>   Well, there'll be a ... a moral
>   obligation for them to help us.
>   They wouldn't deny us assistance
>   once we'd landed on those islands,
>   in spite of what they say.

He indicates Roosevelt's telegram, which he is still
holding.

180. (CONTINUED)

                          BROOKE
                          (bitter)
                    I know for a fact that Marshall
                    hasn't even read the Overlord
                    plan.

                          CHURCHILL
                    Well, he can soon do that.
                    Anyhow, the Command would fall
                    to Eisenhower.

Silence.

                          BROOKE
                    If you will excuse me, sir, I
                    feel desperately tired.

                          CHURCHILL
                          (surprised)
                    Of course, of course, good night.

CHURCHILL dismisses BROOKE with a wave of the hand.
BROOKE starts to go.

                    Oh, Brookie. I suppose you must
                    be a bit disappointed. To lose
                    the Command.

                          BROOKE
                    A bit.

                          CHURCHILL
                    Fortunes of war.

He strikes a match to light a cigar.

BROOKE watches him for a bit, his face illuminated by
the match; then goes.

181. NEWSFILM

Invasion of Italy, September 1943. The amphibious
British and Canadian Divisions of the 8th Army come
in from Sicily under smokescreen, and stream ashore.

                          MONTGOMERY (V.O.)
                    My dear Brookie, I attacked across
                    the Straights of Messina at 04.30
                    hours this morning, and am now
                    well established on the toe of
                    Italy. Opposition slight.

182. NEWSFILM

8th Army armour advancing through the narrow hilly
roads of Calabria. Some opposition.

> ALEXANDER (V.O.)
> Alexander to Prime Minister.
> 8th Army advancing rapidly North.
> Germans fighting small rearguard
> action as they retreat.

183. NEWSFILM

Salerno Landings, September 1943.

5th Army (British and American) storm the beach from
an armada of landing craft, and struggle to obtain a
beachhead.

Heavy fire pounds their advance from shore batteries.

> IKE (V.O.)
> Eisenhower to Joint Chiefs of
> Staff. Fifth Army landed at
> Salerno. Encountering fierce
> opposition. Fear heavy
> casualties.

184. INT. WAR ROOM

A British Chiefs-of-Staff meeting, chaired by BROOKE.

EDEN and ISMAY are also present.

A map of Southern Italy is on the table, with the
5th Army position and 8th Army advance clearly marked.

> BROOKE
> So the question is a simple one.
> Can the 5th Army bridgehead at
> Salerno
> (points)
> hold out until the 8th Army fight
> their way through from the South
> to relieve them ?

> EDEN
> Surely the Salerno garrison can
> be strengthened by sea ?

184.   (CONTINUED)

                         ISMAY
              We have the reinforcements
              waiting in Tunisia but no
              landing craft to ship them
              over.

                         EDEN
              For God's sake, why not ?

                         BROOKE
              Apparently the Americans
              decided to make it impossible
              for us to jettison 'Overlord'
              in favour of an extended
              Mediterranean campaign, by
              withdrawing every landing
              craft they reckoned we could
              do without, before the invasion.

185.   INT. BEDROOM

ISMAY with CHURCHILL, who is in a towering rage.

                         CHURCHILL
              But that is monstrous,
              criminal ! Their own men are
              at Salerno.

                         ISMAY
              The need for reinforcements on
              this scale was not anticipated.

                         CHURCHILL
              Withdraw landing craft, so
              that we can't use them ?

                         ISMAY
                         (dry)
              The result of a loss of trust,
              I daresay.

ON CHURCHILL.

186.   INT. WHITE HOUSE

Darkness. HOPKINS is shaking ROOSEVELT awake.

                         ROOSEVELT
                         (waking)
              What is it ? Harry ?

186.   (CONTINUED)

                                    HOPKINS
                                (with telegram)
                        The Italian Government have
                        accepted the armistice.

        ROOSEVELT grabs the telegram and scans it.

                        The terms are those we
                        proposed.

                                    ROOSEVELT
                        What's the German position ?

                                    HOPKINS
                        They've disarmed the Italians
                        and have taken over the shore
                        defences right down the South
                        West coast, under Field-
                        Marshal Kesselring. That's
                        why the boys at Salerno are
                        having such a rough time.

        ROOSEVELT struggles up onto one elbow, deeply troubled.

                                    ROOSEVELT
                        Isn't there time to get more
                        landing craft up to relieve
                        them ? How far away were they
                        taken ?

                                    HOPKINS
                        Much too far.

187. CLOSE-UPS

        CLOSE-UPS of EISENHOWER, ALEXANDER and MONTGOMERY,
        each on the telephone, having an agitated conference
        by phone.

        EISENHOWER is tremendously upset.

                                    IKE
                        If Salerno turns out a disaster,
                        the casualties will be fearful !

                                    ALEXANDER
                                (to MONTGOMERY)
                        How long will it take you to
                        get through to them now ?

187. (CONTINUED)

                              MONTGOMERY
          Four days.

                                   IKE
          Four ?

188. NEWSFILM

     Salerno. More of a bridgehead established. Fighting
     extremely fierce, with heavy casualties.

                              ALEXANDER (V.O.)
                         Alexander to Prime Minister.
                         Kesselring has abruptly pulled
                         back at Monty's approach, for
                         fear of being trapped between
                         the two armies. Salerno now
                         seems safe.

     German troops in rapid but orderly retreat.

                         Have little doubt they are
                         reforming to launch counter-
                         attack.

189. INT. UNDERGROUND CORRIDOR

     CHURCHILL strides down the long passage, with EDEN.
     His body is now that of a man in his seventieth year,
     but his eyes gleam with the 1940 fire again.

                              CHURCHILL
                         Now is the time to take the
                         Greek Islands ! If there was
                         ever a golden opportunity, it
                         is now !

                              EDEN
                         But we should weigh the
                         advantages of unilateral
                         action, against -

                              CHURCHILL
                         The Italian Government has
                         ordered those islands to come
                         over to us, and they will do so
                         provided we reach them quickly.

189.   (CONTINUED)

> EDEN
> Before the Germans disarm them ?

> CHURCHILL
> Precisely.

Enters Ante Room.

190.   INT.   ANTE ROOM

CHURCHILL bursting into the room.

> CHURCHILL
> General Maitland Wilson has
> reserves of men in Egypt which
> can be shipped across. Pug,
> come in here with us !

He strides through to the War Room, ISMAY and EDEN
following.

191.   INT.   WAR ROOM

> CHURCHILL
> Cable Maitland Wilson in
> Alexandria that he should send
> an expedition forthwith to
> occupy the islands of Rhodes,
> Cos, Leros, Samos ...

> EDEN
> But surely we should consult
> the Americans about this ?

SECRETARY enters, and CHURCHILL starts to dictate
immediately she appears round the door:

> CHURCHILL
> "To General Maitland Wilson,
> Commander-in-Chief, East
> Mediterranean. Begins. Here
> is a matter of great consequence,
> to be thrust forward by every
> means ...

On EDEN and ISMAY, full of apprehension and alarm.

192. <u>INT. H.Q. MIDDLE EAST COMMAND.   COMMANDER-IN-CHIEF'S ROOM</u>

SENIOR OFFICERS crowded round a map of Eastern Mediterranean.
Among them is GENERAL MAITLAND 'JUMBO' WILSON, an
enormously fat and cheerful man, a romantic, with quick
and razor-sharp mind.

> CHURCHILL (V.O.)
> ... I understand you have reserves
> which could be made immediately
> available. Use whatever shipping
> you can muster to cross the
> Mediterranean. Here are immense
> prizes at little cost.

We see CLOSE SHOT of the MAP, with WILSON indicating
the route from Alexandria to Rhodes and the Greek Islands.

> WILSON (V.O.)
> Maitland Wilson to Prime Minister.
> Immediate preparations in hand
> but desperate need for transport
> shipping. All my assault craft
> handed over to Eisenhower last
> month on Admiralty orders.

193. <u>INT. ANTE ROOM</u>

ISMAY and EDEN.

> ISMAY
> He said, "Then use ship's life-
> boats, fishing vessels, anything".

> EDEN
> The distance is too great. And
> if the Germans take Rhodes, we
> shall need landing craft,
> transport aircraft ...

> ISMAY
> All of which are allocated to
> Italy or to 'Overlord'.

EDEN pours over the Greek Islands map. We see how
they dominate the Balkans and Dardenelles.

> EDEN
> I wish to God Winston would
> call the whole thing off.

193. (CONTINUED)

                              ISMAY
          The Americans will stop it.

                              EDEN
          But they don't know about it,
          yet !

                              ISMAY
          You forget - they get copies of
          all Middle East telegrams.

194. WHITE HOUSE. OVAL ROOM

STIMSON walking about the room, exploding with anger.

ROOSEVELT and HOPKINS sit examining copy of a British
military telegram he has given them.

                              STIMSON
          He's going to invade on Thursday !
          He must be senile !

                              ROOSEVELT
          What are his chances ?

                              HOPKINS
          Fifty-fifty, Marshall says.
          Less now the Germans have
          captured Rhodes.

                              STIMSON
          It's directly against our agreed
          policy not to extend the
          Mediterranean war ! - It's
          clearly an attempt to postpone
          'Overlord' yet again !

                              HOPKINS
          I think it's more an attempt to
          relive his Finest Hour. He won't
          accept that 1940 was four damn
          years ago.

                              STIMSON
          We must impose our will, Mr.
          President.

                              ROOSEVELT
          And stop him ?

                              STIMSON
          Yes, sir !

195. <u>INT. WAR ROOM</u>

CHURCHILL and BROOKE, walking about on either side
of the Cabinet table - a hammer-and-tongs row.

                    CHURCHILL
          Within a month, the Balkans
          could be ablaze, and Allied
          troops would be able to attack
          the flank and rear of Germany !
          The war could be over by
          Christmas.

                    BROOKE
          But you haven't the means to
          <u>hold</u> the islands, sir -

                    CHURCHILL
                    (fierce)
          We hadn't the means in 1940,
          but did we flinch ?

                    BROOKE
          In 1940 we didn't have to
          consider the Americans.

                    CHURCHILL
          If I considered them now, they
          would just prevaricate. Alexander
          will help, he will be Supreme
          Commander -

                    BROOKE
          But he isn't yet ! And we're
          invading tomorrow !

196. <u>NEWSFILM</u>

British invasion of the Greek Islands.

Troops being put ashore from a hastily improvised
flotilla of coastal vessels and sailing ships -
Dunkirk in reverse.

                    WILSON (V.O.)
          Maitland Wilson to Prime Minister.
          I today took possession of the
          islands of Leros, Cos and Samos.
          A flight of Spitfires will be
          established here tonight. Local
          defences entirely inadequate,
          and we cannot bring up our own
          heavy weapons from Egypt with
          the meagre shipping at our
          disposal.

197. INT. CHURCHILL'S BEDROOM

CHURCHILL dictating.

>   CHURCHILL
> Prime Minister to General
> Eisenhower. I beg you
> temporarily to lend us enough
> shipping to transport defence
> weapons from Egypt to our new
> Greek Island bases.

198. NEWSFILM

Italian troops on sit-down strike.

>   WILSON (V.O.)
> Maitland Wilson to Prime
> Minister. Italians flatly
> refusing to assist defence of
> Greek Islands. Eisenhower
> must lend us troops !

199. INT. OFFICE IN EISENHOWER'S VILLA, ALGERIA

EISENHOWER dictates, spelling it out with great firmness.

>   IKE
> To Prime Minister Churchill.
> Field-Marshal Kesselring has
> ordered stand South of Rome,
> for decisive battle to drive
> us back into the sea. Unable
> therefore to send any
> assistance.
>   (he throws his arms
>   up in exasperation)
> He must be out of his mind !

200. NEWSFILM

Heavy German paratroop drop to take Cos airfield.

> WILSON (V.O.)
> Maitland Wilson to the Prime
> Minister. German paratroops
> took the island of Cos with
> central airfield today. Regret
> the loss of eight hundred men.

201. INT. CHURCHILL'S BEDROOM

CHURCHILL has been woken up with this dispatch.

He dictates a reply, pounding the bedclothes with his fists.

> CHURCHILL
> Storm Rhodes ! Improvise, and
> dare ! Germans have so far been
> unable to consolidate the island.
> I will somehow get you shipping
> for the operation - but storm
> Rhodes ! To President Roosevelt:
> Surely the provision of a handful
> of landing craft, and ten
> transport aircraft for one week,
> could not embarrass Eisenhower
> in his forthcoming battle !

202. INT. WHITE HOUSE. OVAL ROOM

ROOSEVELT dictating, spelling it out to CHURCHILL with steely resolve.

> ROOSEVELT
> Roosevelt to Prime Minister
> Churchill. In my opinion, no
> diversion of troops or equipment
> should prejudice 'Overlord' as
> planned.

203. <u>INT. WAR ROOM</u>

BROOKE and ISMAY with CHURCHILL, who stands reading
the telegram, shaken and unable to believe it.

                    BROOKE
                   (quietly)
         Do you not think, sir, that
         this leaves us no option but
         a withdrawal ?

                    CHURCHILL
         Withdrawal ? Our boats are
         unarmed, they would be shot out
         of the water !

Silence.

                    ISMAY
         I suppose Eisenhower may lend
         us enough long-range fighters
         to cover an evacuation ?

                    BROOKE
         Roosevelt says "in my opinion".
         That still leaves Eisenhower
         some discretion.

Pause.

                    CHURCHILL
         Cable Eisenhower I am coming to
         see him. Arrange a plane to
         Algiers tonight.

204. <u>INT. OFFICE IN EISENHOWER'S VILLA, ALGERIA</u>

EISENHOWER on telephone to Marshall in Washington.

                    IKE
         I'm leaving in half an hour,
         sir - can't he be stopped ?

205. <u>INT. WHITE HOUSE</u>

                    MARSHALL
         Short of the U.S. Marines
         storming Downing Street, I
         doubt it. I'm just warning you.

206. INT. OFFICE IN EISENHOWER'S VILLA, ALGERIA

                         IKE
               Thank you, sir.

207. INT. WHITE HOUSE

                              MARSHALL
                    I've seen strong men go in to
                    see Churchill determined to say
                    'no', and come out half an
                    hour later meek as new born
                    lambs.

208. INT. FLYING BOAT

CHURCHILL working through papers, but his mind isn't
on them.

He looks away, remembering:

209. STILLS

Gallipoli. The sea full of bodies floating in the
water, hundreds upon hundreds.

Sequence of stills FADING INTO EACH OTHER.

                              ISMAY (V.O.)
                    Sir ?

210. INT. FLYING BOAT

CHURCHILL looks up.

ISMAY is holding out a telegram to him.

                              ISMAY
                    From General Maitland Wilson.
                    Relayed by the War Cabinet
                    Office.

210. (CONTINUED)

CHURCHILL takes telegram and reads it.

TIGHTENING on CHURCHILL.

> WILSON (V.O.)
> German bombing becoming intense.
> Doubtless preliminary to
> invasion. Unless we can get
> air cover and transport, regret
> our position must be seen as
> desperate.

We have arrived at BIG CLOSE UP CHURCHILL.

211. INT. OFFICE. EISENHOWER'S VILLA, ALGIERS

CHURCHILL and EISENHOWER.

> IKE
> (firm and forceful)
> I am sorry that it is not
> possible to help you in the
> Aegean.

> CHURCHILL
> (mock horror)
> You would not abandon us ?

> IKE
> It's not a case of abandoning.

> CHURCHILL
> You would allow military
> catastrophe to overtake your
> closest ally, for want of a
> few ships -

> IKE
> Hardly 'a few'.

> CHURCHILL
> Landing craft for a single
> division, and a few days'
> assistance from the Allied
> Air Force - a tiny fraction
> of your forces !

EISENHOWER suspicious.

211.   (CONTINUED)

                                IKE
                I understood you wanted more
                than that.

                                CHURCHILL
                Indeed ?

                                IKE
                Alexander said something about
                a bombarding force, a hospital
                ship, transport aircraft ...
                Sounded more like an assault
                than an evacuation.

He is watching CHURCHILL closely, unsure of how much
of his hand he has actually disclosed.

                                CHURCHILL
                I would remind you that we
                voluntarily placed all our
                resources in your hands !

                                IKE
                To achieve a common victory.

                                CHURCHILL
                Certainly, certainly.

                                IKE
                The capture of Sicily and
                Southern Italy.

                                CHURCHILL
                My concepts, for which I had
                to fight !

                                IKE
                And you were right.
                        (firm)
                But with the greatest respect,
                sir, you are quite wrong about
                the Aegean.

CHURCHILL is growing angry.

                                CHURCHILL
                I should also remind you that
                until Operation 'Torch' less than
                twelve months ago, you had never
                heard a shot fired in anger !

211.   (CONTINUED)

                              IKE
            Whereas your military career
            spans fifty years.

                          CHURCHILL
            You are aware of that ?

                              IKE
            And I respect it.

                          CHURCHILL
            Indeed ?

                              IKE
            Certainly, of course !

                          CHURCHILL
                    (fresh tack)
            Then surely you see that the
            Italian and Balkan peninsulas
            are militarily and politically
            one ? The Germans certainly
            believe this - why else should
            they take vital air forces away
            from Kesselring to defend them,
            at a time when -

                              IKE
                    (interrupting)
            I feel we should be quite open
            with each other, Mr. Churchill.
            Precisely what do you want of me ?

                          CHURCHILL
            One first class Division, ten
            landing craft, and some aircraft,
            for the capture of Rhodes.

                              IKE
            No, sir !

                          CHURCHILL
            Rhodes is the key to it all.

                              IKE
            Out of the question !

                          CHURCHILL
            There would be ample time to
            return the troops to Italy
            before the German counter-attack.

211. (CONTINUED)

                            IKE
The landing craft are allocated
to 'Overlord'.

                        CHURCHILL
Ten craft out of the five
hundred for 'Overlord' ? -
And six months before they
are needed ?

                            IKE
But you have no intention of
stopping at Rhodes ! - if you
did, the island would be under
the guns of both Cos and Crete,
a hopeless position - we'd have
to take more islands and maybe
even launch a fullscale invasion
of the Balkans to hold it !
Look, sir, I will send you some
long-range fighters to help
evacuate two squadrons for four
days, but that's all I can spare !
       (angry and distressed)
Forgive me, sir, but you can no
longer expect to win this war
by yourself ! Before America
came in, there was no strategy
at all, to speak of - just a
struggle for survival by whatever
hand-to-mouth means you could
scrape together. You became the
symbol of the British will to
fight on to the finish - unquestioned,
magnificent, an act of bravery that
will inspire men for centuries,
wonderful, you could hear it all
in your voice. But those times
are past. This is global war.
And we can no longer base world
strategy on your instinct.

Silence. CHURCHILL in despair at this final 'no'.

                        CHURCHILL
Why is everyone against me ?

                            IKE
We're not against you, sir. But
you've done your part, now.

212. NEWSFILM

The fall of the Greek Islands, under heavy German
air bombardment and amphibious invasion.

> WILSON (V.O.)
> Maitland Wilson to Prime
> Minister. Following withdrawal
> of long-range fighters, have no
> alternative but to order general
> surrender.

213.   INT. CORRIDOR

ISMAY knocks at the part-open door to Churchill's bedroom.

> ISMAY
> Mr. Churchill ?

> CHURCHILL
> (O.O.V.)
> Yes, Pug.

> ISMAY
> Military telegram, sir.

> CHURCHILL
> (O.O.V.)
> Bring it in, bring it in.

213a. INT. CHURCHILL'S BEDROOM

CHURCHILL lying deep in an armchair. For the first time
in the play, he looks an old, tired, despairing, broken
man.

> ISMAY
> From Maitland Wilson, sir.
> Summarising our losses in the
> Greek Islands.

> CHURCHILL
> Yes ?

> ISMAY
> We lost 4 cruisers, 7 destroyers
> and 5,000 men. Many were found
> dead in the water, floating off
> the beaches.

213a. (CONTINUED)

CHURCHILL is so appalled he cannot speak.

In an extraordinary, agonised gesture, he places a
cushion over his head and face, and sinks down into
the armchair.

MIXING, as he does so, to:

213b. <u>STILLS</u>

The Gallipoli drowned, floating in the water.

ACT TWELVE

214. INT. THE HALL OF ST. PAUL'S SCHOOL.
WEST KENSINGTON, LONDON

On stage is an immense map of the Channel, the
Normandy coast and the immediate hinterland,
"set at an angle so the audience may see it clearly,
and so constructed that the high officers explaining
the plan of operations could walk about on it and
explain its landmarks as they speak."

May 1944. A final briefing conference for 'Overlord'.
Every senior officer is present, from all the services -
the KING, CHURCHILL, the ENTIRE WAR CABINET,
CHIEFS-OF-STAFF, GENERALS - the small hall is crammed.

The KING, CHURCHILL, LASCELLES, ADMIRAL RAMSAY,
BROOKE, MONTGOMERY, EDEN, EISENHOWER, ATTLEE, ISMAY.

MONTGOMERY is on the stage, addressing the Conference.

                    MONTGOMERY
          Now I know I am regarded by
          many people as being a tiresome
          person. I think this is very
          likely true. I try hard not to
          be tiresome, but I have seen so
          many mistakes made in this war,
          and so many disasters, I am
          desperately anxious to see we have
          no more. That is why I insisted
          on major revisions to the Overlord
          plan for the invasion of France,
          which I shall now demonstrate.
                    (he does so, with a
                     huge pointer)
          Here is the invasion coast in
          Normandy, divided into sections,
          Utah, Omaha, Gold, Juno and Sword.
          The British force will land on
          the Eastern sector here, here and
          here ...

214. (CONTINUED)

>   MONTGOMERY
>   (cont'd - indicates
>   Gold, Juno and Sword)
>   .... and push South East towards
>   Caen. The Americans will land at
>   the base of the Cherbourg
>   Peninsula here and here ...
>   (Utah and Omaha)
>   ... and secure Cherbourg itself.
>   There they will build up their
>   forces for a breakout ...

We have been PANNING OVER the assembled dignitaries
during this, and SETTLED ON CHURCHILL, looking old
and desperately tired, his eyes glazed.

214a. INT.   HALL OF ST. PAUL'S SCHOOL - LATER

EISENHOWER now on stage.

>   IKE
>   The French coast has been
>   precisely surveyed, and solutions
>   devised for each obstacle. Chief
>   of Technical Operations will
>   describe these to you in detail
>   this afternoon.

BROOKE and ISMAY both glance at CHURCHILL; so does
the KING.

The Old Man has suddenly perked up, eyes gleaming.

They are unable to see why.

>   There are assembled in Southern
>   England and on the coast 1,200
>   fighting ships; 4,000 assault
>   craft; 1,600 merchant vessels;
>   13,000 aircraft and three-and-
>   a-half million men. I guess it
>   is only the great number of
>   barrage balloons floating in
>   British skies that are keeping
>   this island afloat.

Laughter.

215. INT. HALL OF ST. PAUL'S SCHOOL - LATER

ADMIRAL RAMSAY now on stage.

                              RAMSAY
                    The Navy's task is to carry the
                    Army safely across the Channel
                    and support the landing by every
                    available means.

CHURCHILL now sits there with a broad grin on his
face, mystifying everyone.

                    Thereafter, it will ensure the
                    arrival of reinforcements and
                    supplies. There are two Naval
                    Task Forces - the Eastern will
                    command all Naval operations in
                    the British section, and the
                    Western, the American. Each
                    command contains five assault
                    forces ...

216. EXT. GARDENS OF ST. PAULS SCHOOL

BROOKE and EDEN sit round a large wicker basket,
covered with a tablecloth, eating a picnic lunch.
There is a third plate and chair for Churchill,
unoccupied.

OTHER OFFICERS may be seen lunching on other parts
of the flat roof in the sunshine.

                              BROOKE
                    I do hope someone will underline
                    the weak points of the plan this
                    afternoon.

                              EDEN
                    I don't think any responsible
                    person has considered what would
                    happen if it should fail.

                              BROOKE
                    It doesn't bear thinking about.
                    But it's perfectly possible.

Pause.

                    Were you talking to Winston ?

216. (CONTINUED)

> EDEN
>
> No ?

> BROOKE
>
> He's up to something.

CHURCHILL hurries back, and sits down to his lunch.

> CHURCHILL
>
> My dear Anthony, my dear
> Brookie, I do beg your pardon.
> I just had to have a word with
> Admiral Ramsay.

CHURCHILL tucks into his food with relish, and with an audible chuckle.

EDEN and BROOKE exchange mystified glances.

217. INT. HALL ST. PAUL'S SCHOOL

CHURCHILL addressing the Conference, with his old spirit.

> CHURCHILL
>
> There is no sign that the enemy
> has penetrated our vast secret.
> But continued secrecy is
> imperative - all papers must be
> marked 'Secret' and 'Top Secret'.
> I am glad to learn that even the
> Senior Padre for this operation
> marks his 'Sacred' and 'Top Sacred'.

Laughter.

> The hour of our greatest effort
> and action is at hand. When the
> signal is given, the whole circle
> of avenging nations will hurl
> themselves upon the foe, and batter
> out the life of the cruellest
> tyranny which has ever sought to
> bar the progress of mankind.
> Gentlemen, we are discussing
> nothing less than the end of
> this war.

217. (CONTINUED)

CHURCHILL sits. Applause, but subdued and thoughtful.

The KING rises to take the platform, and everyone stands.

                    KING
          Please be seated, gentlemen.

They sit.

          I have known of the existence
          of the plan to invade Europe
          since its first conception.
          But I am still still staggered
          at the sheer magnitude of it all.
          I have been visiting each of
          the assult forces at their
          points of assembly ...

218. NEWSFILM

The gigantic preparations for D-Day all over England.

                    KING (V.O.)
          This mighty host is tense as a
          coiled spring - a great human
          spring, coiled for the moment,
          when its energy will be released,
          and it will vault the English
          Channel in the greatest military
          operation ever thought out in the
          world !

219. INT. THE KING'S STUDY

The KING and CHURCHILL, serving themselves at a light
buffet luncheon.

                    KING
          Tell me, Winston, where will you
          be on D-Day itself ?

He eats.

CHURCHILL gives a guilty little start.

219. (CONTINUED)

>   CHURCHILL
>   Well, erm, ah ... actually
>   (he swallows hard)
>   I'm going in with one of the
>   bombardment ships. In the
>   first assault.

The KING is astonished.

>   It's perfectly safe, sir - I've
>   worked it all out with Admiral
>   Ramsay.

He sees the KING's expression

>   Surely you wouldn't have me stay
>   in London doing nothing, sir ?

>   KING
>   You assure me that it's
>   perfectly safe ?

>   CHURCHILL
>   Oh, perfectly, absolutely.

>   KING
>   Good. Then I shall come too.

>   CHURCHILL
>   (horrified)
>   Oh, no, sir, no ! Absolutely
>   out of the question !

>   KING
>   In that case, neither of us
>   shall go.

>   CHURCHILL
>   Oh, but -

>   KING
>   (very firm)
>   Neither of us, Winston.

CHURCHILL bows his head and eventually nods.

>   CHURCHILL
>   Of course, sir.

He flaps his arms, the very picture of misery and
disappointment.

>   But why must I always - throughout
>   the entire war - stay at home,
>   and do nothing !

220.   NEWSFILM

Dusk. Final preparations for the D-Day landings,
the evening before.

The KING's broadcast can be HEARD relayed over landing
craft loudspeakers, radios, wirelesses in canteens
and messes, every domestic wireless in the British
Isles.

                              KING   (V.O.)
                    Four years ago, our Nation
                    and Empire stood alone, with
                    our backs to the wall. Tested
                    as never before in our history,
                    we survived the test; the spirit
                    of the people, resolute,
                    dedicated, burned like a bright
                    flame, lit surely from those
                    Unseen Fires which nothing can
                    quench.

221.   INT. KING'S STUDY

The BBC microphones set up on his desk.

                              KING
                    Now once more a supreme test
                    has to be faced. At this historic
                    moment, surely not one of us is
                    too busy, too young or too old,
                    to play a part in the nationwide,
                    worldwide vigil of prayer, as our
                    great Crusade sets forth.

222.   NEWSFILM

D-Day preparations.

Ships slipping anchor, aeroplanes being checked, rifles
being cleaned and loaded.

                              KING   (V.O.)
                    If from every place of worship,
                    from home and factory, from men
                    and women of all ages and many
                    races and occupations, our
                    intercession rises, then, please
                    God, the predictions of an
                    ancient Psalm may be fulfilled ...

223. <u>INT. WAR ROOM</u>

CHURCHILL sits alone, listening to the broadcast.
Tears are streaming down his face.

The King has for once conquered his stammer, and his
voice rings out with the confidence of battle -

                    KING (V.O.)
          "The Lord will give his strength
          unto this people; the Lord will
          give this people the blessing
          of peace."

224. <u>NEWSFILM</u>

With a thunderous roar, the D-Day bombardment and
aerial attack begins.

Forces of a magnitude never before assembled, and
over a million men, go into action.

                    CHURCHILL   (V.O.)
          In the early hours of this
          morning, British and American
          forces landed on the shores of
          occupied France. Nothing can
          now hold back the flood of
          military might pouring across
          France towards Germany. Do not
          despair, brave Norwegians.
          Your land will be cleansed.
          Be sure of yourselves; Czechs,
          your independence will be restored.
          Poles, the heroism of your people
          standing up to cruel oppressors
          shall not be forgotten. Lift
          up your heads, gallant Frenchmen.
          Tough, stouthearted Dutch,
          Belgians, Luxemburgers. Tormented,
          mishandled, shamefully cast away
          people of Yugoslavia. Glorious
          Greece, yield not an inch !
          Mighty forces are advancing on
          your behalf. Have faith. Have
          hope. Deliverance is sure !

225.   INT.   HALL OF ST. PAUL'S SCHOOL

The huge planning map is now being used as an
'operational position' map, with counters and lines
of tape showing position of British, American and
German lines.

CHURCHILL is watching, gloomy and silent. Three
or four other OFFICERS stand about, miserable that
this is the closest they can get to the action.

Military telegrams come in to the CHIEF ADMINISTRATION
OFFICER, who supervises the staff moving the counters.
There is an air of calm unreality.

BROOKE comes up to CHURCHILL, excited.

                    BROOKE
          There's been a cable from
          Alexander, sir. We've taken
          Rome.

                    CHURCHILL
                 (pause)
          The Mediterranean war is out
          of date. It's quite irrelevant
          now.

BROOKE looks at him, astonished, but says nothing.

He indicates the map.

                    BROOKE
          The beachhead's holding ?

                    CHURCHILL
          Oh yes. Let's go outside, I
          can't bear it in here.

226.   SCENE OMITTED

227.   EXT.   GARDENS OF ST. PAUL'S SCHOOL

A high flat roof, with panoramic view over London.

CHURCHILL and BROOKE are looking upwards at an immense
body of bombers which can be heard roaring overhead.

227. (CONTINUED)

> CHURCHILL
> What are they ?

> BROOKE
> They must be the Cherbourg
> Peninsula force. Softening
> up the 14th Panzers before
> the Americans try the break-
> out.

> CHURCHILL
> (bitter)
> "And gentlemen in England now
> abed, Shall think themselves
> accursed they were not here ..."

> BROOKE
> You know the King's ADC stowed
> away in a bombardment ship,
> and saw the attack ?

> CHURCHILL
> (furious)
> He what ? With us stuck here
> at home, doing nothing ?

228. INT. HALL ST. PAUL'S SCHOOL

We see the counters being moved about on the American
1st Army front, MIXING with NEWSFILM.

> MONTGOMERY (V.O.)
> Montgomery to Joint Chiefs-of-
> Staff. Cherbourg Peninsula
> now cleared ready for break-out
> south of British position,
> towards Paris.

229. EXT. GARDENS ST. PAUL'S SCHOOL

CHURCHILL continuing to pour out wrath against the
King's ADC.

229. (CONTINUED)

                              CHURCHILL
          It's not that he should tell
          to his grandchildren, but what
          we did here ! We stood alone
          for one whole year, and gained
          the time for the good cause to
          organise, and slowly bring the
          irresistable forces of outraged
          civilisation to bear upon the
          criminal - that is our greatest
          glory !

                              BROOKE
          People are aware of that, sir.

                              CHURCHILL
                         (gloomy)
          People soon forget.

                              BROOKE
          You saw the newspapers this
          morning ?

                              CHURCHILL
          About D-Day ?

                              BROOKE
          Yes, but one had a huge picture
          of you on the front page.

                              CHURCHILL
                         (dull)
          Indeed.

                              BROOKE
          In the middle of the Blitz,
          arms raised over your head,
          like this.
                         (he demonstrates)
          Over the top it said, "The
          beginning of the End", and
          underneath, "We love him, and
          we owe him everything".

CHURCHILL is immensely moved and tickled by this.

He purrs, growls, chuckles and blinks back tears
all at once.

230. <u>NEWFILM</u>

The break-out. An immense surge of American armour
on the Eastern flank breaks clean through the German
lines.

> MONTGOMERY (V.O.)
> Montgomery to Joint Chiefs-of-
> Staff. Break-out completely
> successful. American 1st and
> 3rd Armies have smashed through
> German lines and driving hard
> at Paris !

231. <u>INT. HALL ST. PAUL'S SCHOOL</u>

The counters are moved to show the break-out, on the
long but direct line to Berlin.

232. <u>EXT. GARDENS ST. PAUL'S SCHOOL</u>

CHURCHILL muttering to himself, "We love him and we
owe him everything" several times, chuckling and
walking about.

He abruptly starts to sing, not very loud, and
distinctly quavery:

> CHURCHILL
> "I went in to pay the bill
> But instead I took the till,
> My wife and kids were starving ..."

233. <u>NEWSFILM</u>

The Break-out.

American armour streaming towards Germany in immense
force.

234 - <u>EXT. GARDENS ST. PAUL'S SCHOOL</u>

CHURCHILL suddenly raises both arms in the air,
hat, stick and cigar, full 1940 style, and roars
aloud with delight.

FREEZE FRAME

FADE OUT

<u>T H E   E N D</u>